Before They Were Our Mothers

Partial funding for this project provided by Saratoga Arts with a Community Arts Grant from the New York State Council on the Arts with the support of Governor Andrew Cuomo and the New York State Legislature.

SARATOGA ARTS
experience . discover . create

Photos used by permission of authors.

Printed in the United States of America.

Journal Arts Press • Saratoga Springs, New York

For readings, presentations, book stocking, or group sales, contact B4TheyWereOurMothers@gmail.com or visit www.journalartspress.com.

ISBN: 978-0-578-19949-8

Library of Congress Control Number: 2017962746

Before They Were Our Mothers:

Voices of Women Born Before Rosie Started Riveting

Patricia A. Nugent, Editor

Our Stories of Their Stories

Forward
The Story Behind the Book

A tall, stately man showed up at my mother's funeral with mementoes of their time together in high school, more than seventy years prior. I didn't know she'd been the star of her high school play or that she'd had a German shepherd as a child. Or, as I would later discover after finding her diary, that this man had broken her heart when he took up with, and married, her then-best friend. My mother had never mentioned Eugene to me.

After my book about adult parental loss was published, some distant relatives contacted me to share family photographs. I was delighted to see a photo of my grandparents' 1906 wedding. But when I turned it over, a penciled scrawl read, *She didn't love him – was engaged to someone else.* My relatives couldn't identify the commentator, and I was unable to track down more information.

When I told friends of these two incidents, they shared stories they'd learned about their own mothers after they'd died. *Why didn't we know more about these women, so central to our lives? Why were we surprised that our mothers had lives before we came along? Before they were our mothers.*

As a youth, I'd been too consumed with my own drama to care about my foremothers' journeys. And they were proud, private women, not willing to show vulnerability, not wanting to boast.

Perhaps out of regret, perhaps to make sure others don't make the same mistake of not asking or not listening, I conceived of an anthology that would encourage daughters and granddaughters to learn more about the women who'd carried them. The women who had transmitted their bloodline and heritage, who nurtured them, who paved the way for women today to proudly tell their own stories, to speak their truth.

A grant from Saratoga Arts through the New York State Council on the Arts gave me the impetus to proceed. The *Call for Submissions* reaped a wide-range of stories about foremothers' victories and defeats, hopes and disappointments, connections and alienations. Stories of ordinary lives contending with war, racism, sexism, classism, disease, poverty, and degradation. Ordinary lives infused with determination and defiance, resilience and resistance. Ordinary lives of women who will henceforth inspire us – and make us realize women have been contending with, and transcending, cultural, social, and political failings for a very long time.

This anthology also offers a personal history of world events from the late 1800s to the mid-1900s, as seen through the eyes of the women who lived it, as written by their current-day descendants. Their stories take us around the world: Canada, France, Great Britain, Ireland, Italy, Portugal, Russia, Sweden, Ukraine and, in the United States, Minnesota, New York, Pennsylvania, and the Deep South. Universal themes weave delicate threads through these disparate women's lives: Well-meaning parents making questionable decisions; arranged marriages; the desire for education and a career; unplanned pregnancies; the centrality of faith and religion; immigration; the need for affiliation and affirmation; healing and medical advances; the brutality of war; and the crippling effects of prejudice and discrimination. Themes still prevalent in our lives today.

I marvel at the synchronicity of these randomly-collected stories: Penicillin, the new miracle drug, saves one girl's life and kills another's father. While a woman studies miners' work conditions, a girl loses her father to talc-related lung disease. War provides opportunity for some, yet horrific loss for others. Frequent references to moving-picture shows and the railroad add to the nostalgic tone of these real-life tales.

It's my privilege to help bring these stories – these women – to life. They will haunt us, as we see ourselves and people we know. We're left wondering what became of ax-swinging Mary, where Maria's family went after eviction by the priest, and if Dorothy married Dick. We become invested in their fates because good stories make us want to know more. And these are good stories, based on real circumstances.

My ongoing vision is that this book will be a catalyst for storytelling and truth-telling within families. In particular, women's stories, which are too-often silenced or drowned out. Ask now, before it's too late. You won't be able to *Google* the story of Grandma's first heartbreak.

Patricia A. Nugent, Editor

Native Born
by Rachael Z. Ikins

Julia Ophelia Dawson Smith (1849-1930)

I slap a mosquito from my neck. My hand comes away bloody. "Julia Ophelia Dawson Smith," I say to myself, as tears well up in my eyes. "Don't you cry over a dumb bug." I smear it onto an already-dirty skirt.

Feels like years since we left Alabama.

Mama had explained that some men had itchy feet. I had married one. Richmond is a good husband, but yearns for the frontier life, open skies. War decided him to pack everything onto this wagon where I now sway. He tied the heifer behind, stowed our trunks inside with barely room for us to stretch out, and hitched the mule.

Westward, ho!

Sulfur scent of rotting vegetation means we're close to the Red River. We've struggled through war-torn country. Crossing the Mississippi was scary in a thunderstorm. Once we reach the west bank of the Red, we'll be in Texas.

Mama's back in Alabama.

Pain lances my swollen belly. Starts in my lower spine, then arcs around the front, same place as apron strings. It sure doesn't feel like my monthlies. My eyes brim again. I glance at other wagons jostling toward the river. My old life vanishing with each mile. Rich bought a stake in Texas, figures it's a big place, safe.

I listen to pots jangling, curses as a horse refuses to budge, someone's dismayed shout – a bag fallen off a wagon. I lean out, shading my eyes with one hand, the other on the small of my back. I see socks and shifts trampled into the mud. Such a waste, all the work darning and sewing. My heart goes out to the woman who made them.

Mixed with my clothes are baby gowns hand-stitched by friends. Mama had given a party. Invited neighbors, church friends, and relatives who lived close enough. They brought cobblers and pies – blueberry, strawberry rhubarb, and my favorite, peach, set on trestles in the yard. The men gathered down at the barn, smoking and exclaiming over the size of the hogs. Clapping Rich on the back, though I wondered why. He didn't do anything difficult. I'm the one with an aching back, sore breasts, and swelling feet.

At last, after years of hoping.

Children had darted among adults. They pitched a clay ball back and forth, swinging at it with a stick. When I opened my gifts, I'd marveled over the intricate designs embroidered on the small caps.

I lean against the wagon frame, close my eyes. Pain again. The baby's been quiet the past day. Before, he kicked up a storm, especially at night when I struggled to find a comfortable position to sleep. Tonight, we'll camp near the river; tomorrow, we'll cross.

I've no appetite for jerky, cornbread, and beans. Just thinking about food nauseates me, as will floating across another rushing river.

Another pain grips me. I shift in my seat. A gush of warm wetness drenches my thighs, soaks my skirts. Mama had told me that means the baby's ready to come.

I debate telling Rich, glancing sideways at his stubbly cheeks, long nose, and pursed lips. He concentrates, guiding the mule.

"Whoa!" he exclaims, pulling the reins. He smiles, "Think this'll do us."

He leans close to kiss my chapped lips. Neither of us has bathed in a while. I barely notice smells anymore. He hops off, stretches, his back bones popping, and ground-ties the mule.

"I'll fetch some grain and start a fire, honey. Y'all need help jumping down?"

How like a man to ask a nine-month-pregnant and in-labor woman if she needs help jumping off a six-foot-high wagon! I sigh, "Yes, please." His muscled arms grab mine. He sets me on my feet. I groan.

"Feelin' poorly?" His arm encircles my shoulders, as his other hand pats the pocket where he keeps the waxed paper with the map to our land.

"Richmond," I whisper. "Baby's comin'."

"Here? Julie, not 'til we are across! You sure?"

"Babies come when they want. Don't care about stakes or rivers. I'm sure. My water's broke." I hug my middle.

Rich's eyes dart around the growing crowd: Freed slaves, soldiers, Cherokees, farm families. The whites of his eyes remind me of a spooked horse. I toe the mud with one boot, my hand plucking at my brown homespun skirt.

This is new to us both.

"You could walk through the camp and see if there's maybe a woman to help me."

"You bet!" He claps his brimmed floppy hat on the red hair that matches his eyebrows. Off he strides.

I pant, bend my knees. It helps. I walk around the wagon like I've seen cows walk through their birth pangs.

Dusk coalesces from sunset sky and brings hordes of hungry mosquitoes. I want to cry, but why bother.

"I sure wish you could have waited," I murmur. Back home, friends and sage ladies speculated on the sex of my offspring. Depending on how high I carried or how active the baby. I figure it's a boy, no matter what anyone predicts. Just like a male to pick the bank of a bug-filled river far from home to show up.

With great difficulty, I haul myself back into the wagon to search for our sleeping pallet. Pain sucks my breath away. I exhale – *whoosh*. My heart pounding, I rest, sweaty head on forearms. Black flies whine. Pain eases. I unroll the pallet, smooth it, pull a quilt from a basket. Having long ago given up on having a child, I struggle to remember everything Mama told me. I lie on my side panting, one arm over my eyes. As my mind wanders, I realize with a shock that today is my birthday. I am now forty years old.

Where is Rich? Surely, he could find a woman who might help! I sit up, elbows on knees. I make out his anxious tones from the camp noises – horses jingling, grain crunching, people talking, cook fires crackling. I breathe a prayer of thanks, a woman's voice answers. Next thing, Rich pulls aside the wagon cover to help an older lady step up.

"There you are! Honey, this is Miz Lula. My wife, Julia."

The woman has gray-streaked brown hair in a braid and

wrinkles around her eyes, as if she spends a lot of time laughing. Her skin is sun-browned. Rimless spectacles perch on her nose. She looks like an angel.

"Howdy, young lady. Baby comin'?"

I nod. Miz Lula eases her plump body down. It's a tight fit.

A griddle overhead knocks her bonnet. She instructs Rich to take buckets, fetch water, hang a pail over the fire. I pant out puffs of air. Miz Lula stuffs her bonnet into a nearby basket.

"I'm not too old for a first baby? I gave up long since."

She smiles, hands on her knees. "Honey, babies come into this world every day. Have since before Mary birthed the Baby Jesus. You can do this. Not too old. Let me feel your belly and between your legs so I can figure out when this baby is fixin' to join us. Roll on your back; let your knees fall apart."

I study Miz Lula's face as her gentle fingers probe. Her skin is dark. As if she read my mind, she says, "I'm half Cherokee. My daddy was a trapper come west after beaver, and my mama was a full-blood squaw. I grew up in her village."

Miz Lula distracts me, prattling about this and that.

"Can you tell me how much time between pains?" she asks as she wipes her hands on her apron. "If you don't know, let's count when the next one starts."

"Alright." I push my hair off my forehead. A pain begins. I look at her. We count together: "One, two, three, four." Pausing to breathe, I tense as the next one claws my middle. "One, two, three, four." Feels like I have a boulder stuck inside my female parts. A long time since I had a normal-sized body.

"Baby's comin' shortly," Lula declares. "Sit up against this trunk, darlin'. Pull your legs to your chest. Ain't nobody here but us two." As she says it, she plumps the quilt and shoves it between me and the metal trunk clasps. I whisper through clenched teeth, "Thank you."

Pains close in. Lula helps me squat over the pallet. I can't imagine doing such a thing, but her strong arms know what to tell my body. "Next time, go ahead and push, hard as you can." She brushes hair out of my eyes.

"One, two, three!"

My body has a will of its own. Muscles strain. I whimper. Lula says, "I see the head. Red hair!"

Oh my, I think, and push until I feel as if my eyeballs will pop. I feel the head. Lula urges, "Go on, girl!"

"Huhhhnn!"

Her hand slips inside me to ease out one shoulder, then the other.

Rich is outside, scared to death, I know. "You okay, Julie?"

I gasp.

A tiny new voice wails outrage to the world.

Richmond enters just in time to see Miz Lula lay a perfect baby boy on my breasts. "You have a son."

We give him his daddy's middle name. Would be Ophelia if a girl. "I knew you were a boy, Carter. You sure came at the worst time."

Lula nudges the baby's face closer to my breasts. "Let him suck. First milk that comes is clear, and it's 'specially important. But bein' forty, you mightn't make enough milk. I heard of a former slave here in camp, her baby died. Could maybe help wet-nurse."

To gain your freedom but lose your child seems unbearable. Heartbreaking.

When Carter feels the nipple, he pulls it into his mouth. I nickname him *Crawdad*. He sure is strong. Rich strokes my hair, reaches a hand to touch his son.

Through the night, while Carter was getting himself born, dawn came and went, windy with promise of storms. Camp bustles. Folks line up to begin crossing. Some of the mules sound unhappy. A wagon tips over. Men shout as trunks and clothes float away. Helpers splash into the waves to capture a thrashing horse.

Confident, his son born safe, Rich crams a piece of dry corn pone into his mouth and rushes to batten down anything loose. It's our turn. He rolls the canvas sides up and ties them so they'll stay dry. A Cherokee guide stands up to his ankles in the rushing water, calls to the mule. Rich saws on the reins, clucks his tongue. Up to its belly, the animal throws its head. "Ho!" shouts Rich. The brave urges the mule on. The current takes us, mule swimming hard, snorts as waves knock his face.

Louisiana now behind us. Unknown awaits.

Miz Lula cleans me up while Carter sleeps in a basket. Wagon rocks like a boat on the ocean. "Your face is green. Seasick, I bet," she tells me.

My belly is still huge. She assures me this is normal after a baby, but I can see on her face there's more to it. Pain lances my middle. Sweat springs out on my forehead. Water slaps the wagon.

"Honey, you have another baby comin'. We got to get ready. You're an expert now. Second'll be easy."

I don't know whether to laugh or cry. Twins. I'm so tired. No sleep last night, and here we are bouncing through a river's strong current like an apple in a bobbing game.

"I thought I was barren," I gasp. Most friends my age are grandmas. Miz Lula braces my back. I take a breath. "One, two, three!"

My face feels red as sunburn. My legs draw up on their own.

"Push!"

Richmond hears none of this over the river noise. Suddenly, the wagon feels different. Mule must've touched bottom. I see Rich pat his vest for that waxed packet and hear him slap the reins. I bet he's thinking *Texas, almost home.* Heifer lows, eager for landfall, too. Men grab us as we clear the waves. Then thunder booms. I hope the mule is too spent to care. Rich wipes his face with a sleeve. I'm happy for the breeze that slips under the canvas, soothing my hot cheeks. He guides the wagon to a nearby stand of young poplar trees, all the while checking his map. He talks low to the livestock. We set out again. Storm passes.

The sun dips, light, a bright pinkish-orange. River's long gone, feels like a hundred miles ago. We stop. He sets the brake and climbs down, like an old man. "Truth be told," he tells me later, "the whole time we were on the water, I almost forgot to breathe."

He staggers to the back of the wagon, telling me this is our place, and hears Miz Lula say, "Push!" Startled, he watches a second small body slip into the world.

I smile through tears as the baby fusses, waking his identical twin brother. Miz Lula cleans and swaddles him. I mumble, "Rich, we have twins. Our first-born Texan. Can we name him Walter?"

Homesick, I miss Mama so much in this moment. I can't forget that woman whose baby passed, either. I waited so long for mine. Miz Lula wraps the afterbirth in cloth.

"Can you help me out of the wagon? I want to be in open air."

Lula and Rich brace me and help me down. I sniff the breeze, sweet with the scent of blue flowers everywhere. Poplar leaves whisper. Ground beneath my boots is sandy.

Home.

"Let me have that bundle, please." I will dig a hole, bury the afterbirth like a seed – all four of us are part of its contents – the seed of our family, on our land.

I sink to my knees. Rich holds my shoulders. I touch my lips to the loam, kissing good earth.

"Thank you, Lord," I murmur. "For a safe journey to Anna, Texas." I dig with my hands, pulling soil onto my lap. Hard on my knees, but I've just been through harder. I lay the bundle deep, smooth dirt over, pat it. My husband kneels beside me. Earth feels warm, like a baby's back.

Rich promises to find that poor woman who'd lost her baby, figure out how we can help each other.

Two small voices add song to the mockingbirds whistling in the trees. Rich offers me a hand up.

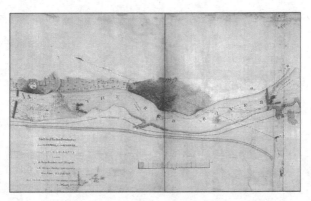

Library of Congress, Geography and Map Division.

Rachael Z. Ikins: The story of my pregnant great-grandmother, bumping west in a wagon across many states, had forever lingered in my consciousness. I'm proud to be related to this strong, resilient woman. At age 19, I went to Texas, knelt at her grave where she was buried at 81 years of age, and scooped some earth into a small bottle. I carried that bottle with me for years. Writing this gave me a sense of roots and competence. I'm a 2016 Pushcart Prize and 2013 CNY Book Award nominee. I've released eight poetry collections and a novel, with three different publishers. I've been a featured poet at Caffe Lena and at Palace Poetry. I live in Baldwinsville, NY.

Horse Thief
by Constance A. Dodge

Mary Adeline Loomis (1899-1983)

On the first day of school, each student was told to stand and say their full name. In front of the twenty-eight students in our one-room schoolhouse, I proudly stand and, in a strong voice, announce, "My name is Mary Loomis."

A silence falls over the room until an older boy hisses, "Horse thief."

I feel the slow burn of humiliation flushing my face. My mind screams, *I am not a horse thief!*

Then I hear my six-year old brother mumble, just above a whisper, "My name is George Washington Loomis."

"Horse thief" echoes around the room until the teacher demands silence.

Miss Hamilton warns the culprits, "You will stay after school today, and for the rest of the week, if you bother the Loomis children or anyone else." This temporarily silences taunts from the older students.

After school, George and I begin our four-mile hike home. The heat of Indian summer makes it seem like a very long time since we left home this morning to walk through the dew-covered pastures. We stop for a moment, and I ask George, "Are you alright after being treated so badly in school?"

His sad eyes meet mine as he answers, "I felt like crying, but I had to be brave."

"Me, too," I respond. "I felt so ashamed. We'll have to ask Pop why someone would try to humiliate us on our first day at our new school."

Our lives have changed so much since May 1907 when my family left the Canadian wilderness to return to central New York State. Many of our cousins live near Oriskany Falls, Waterville, and Sangerfield, the original Loomis homestead by the Nine Mile Swamp. I love our new farm with its mammoth barn and large loft to jump and tumble in the hay – but only after chores. I do wish Mother would give us a little more playtime.

Running excitedly to the crest of the hill, we can see the farm below. I catch up to George as we rush through the gate to find Pop.

"I'll check the barn," I tell my brother.

We spot him in the field past the barnyard. We race to where he's watering our beautiful team of chestnut draft horses. With all the courage I can muster, I describe our day and ask, "Pop, why would anyone call us horse thieves?"

He frowns and, after a brief pause, replies, "Let's sit on the front porch to talk. Mary, please pump a pitcher of water so we can all be refreshed. You must be as thirsty as I am."

Our father puts the horses in the pasture, then walks to his favorite chair on the porch. I hand him a glass of water before sitting on the steps with my brother. Each of us drinks deeply before Pop begins the saga of our ancestral history, starting with Joseph Loomis who left England in 1639. He immigrated to the New England colonies in Windsor Locks, Connecticut.

Then Pop skips ahead several generations to the latter part of the eighteenth century. "Your great, great grandfather, Daniel Loomis, fought in the Revolutionary War."

"Well, that's something we can be proud of," I sing out.

"Daniel must have been honored to serve with General George Washington, Commander of the Continental Army, since he named his son after him." Pop looks at George, and says, "Son, that's why your name is George Washington Loomis, in tribute to your great, great grandfather." A broad grin spreads across my brother's face.

"Unfortunately, at the beginning of the nineteenth century, Daniel's son, George, began stealing horses and running them north into Vermont. A sheriff stopped him in his tracks but was lenient when he realized George was an inexperienced, nineteen-year-old rogue. He swore if he ever caught George stealing horses again, he'd hang him from a tree."

Horse thief, I sigh.

"So, young George – your great grandfather and would-be thief – decided to travel west into New York in search of his cousins. After staying with them and becoming acquainted with the Sangerfield area, he bought a large tract of land that included the legendary Nine Mile Swamp.

"When he met the beautiful and flirtatious Rhoda Millet, he was enamored by her beauty and charm. After a brief courtship, her father gave them permission to marry. Rhoda always boasted that her family belonged to the French aristocracy, exclaiming, 'We were fortunate to escape the guillotine during the French Revolution by sailing off to America.'"

My eight-year-old mind dreams of having my great grandmother's beauty and charm.

"George and Rhoda built a cabin on a slope overlooking their farm. Their family grew quickly, and their highly-intelligent children did well in school. Their son, George Washington, the infamous *Wash*, was especially brilliant and articulate. After completing high school, he studied law with Judge Burton in nearby Hamilton. That gave him the skills he needed to help family members when they were in trouble with the law – which they always were," he added, "because Rhoda taught all her children to steal."

George and I look at each other in amazement that any mother would teach her children to sin. Mother had warned us: *Never take something that belongs to another person because it's against the law and a sin in God's eyes.* Since she's related to a Catholic bishop, it isn't surprising she taught us right from wrong.

"My father, Theodore Wheeler, told me his brothers and sister, Cornelia, stole from the rich to give to the poor, something like Robin Hood."

Does that make it alright to steal things? Mother wants us to understand that we must be responsible for our actions.

I feel disgusted as I listen to Pop tell a story about his uncles stealing a pig from a farmer by convincing him the animal had escaped from their wagon. I know how hard Pop works on the farm, where livestock represents food or barter. I know Pop has never stolen a thing in his life. My great uncles must have been very bad men to rob food from a farmer's family.

I'm lost in my thoughts when Pop resumes his tale. "Most of the time they stole horses and hid them in the Nine Mile Swamp. Loomis Gang members used hot potatoes to create a dappled look on white horses or dyes to transform the colors beyond recognition even to the original owners."

My head is spinning with so many tales about which I can feel anything but pride. I have a queasy sensation in my stomach as I look at the fearful expression on my little brother's face.

"And then there was my Aunt Cornelia," Pop continues. "She was a pretty woman, attracting attention from many young suitors. She and her brothers, with their fine manners and good looks, were often invited to parties in Waterville. After one of these parties, a dozen ladies' fur muffs, essential for keeping your hands warm in a sleigh, were missing. The theft became the talk of Waterville. Many suspected the Loomis boys. So, they planned another party to see if they might catch the culprit.

"Invitations were sent for a Saturday in late January. While everyone was dancing, Cornelia made her way into the ladies' cloakroom. The hostess, Sara, and her friends paused before following her in. The muffs were missing! Sara pushed Cornelia who, caught by surprise, fell backward onto the bed, causing her dress and undergarments to fly up, exposing at least ten muffs, five per leg. A humiliated Cornelia uttered embarrassed apologies as she undressed her limbs. She knew she'd never be invited to a Waterville party again."

Even though that story was very funny, I thought about how George and I had been tormented in school for being associated with these thieves from decades ago. We inherited this shame over things done by people we never even knew.

Our dreadful family history lesson continues. "My uncle, Wash Loomis, the ringleader of the gang, was fatally beaten in 1865 by Constable Filkins and his Midnight Riders. My father, Theodore Wheeler Loomis, then moved to the Watertown area to escape the law. Along with horse thieving, he was accused of attacking and hurting a young woman, which caused lawmen to continue to search for him. In 1880, I was your age, George, when my father moved our large family to Canada. He dropped the name Loomis and began to go by the name Theodore Wheeler instead."

Mother had shown me her marriage certificate with Pop's name written as *Denio Wheeler*. That now made sense to me; another unspoken question was answered. Pop started using Loomis as his last name when our family returned to New York after leaving Canada.

"I still feel the shame," Pop admitted, "of having a father who hurt a young lady's reputation."

I felt shame along with him. And yet, despite all he was revealing, Pop's clannish advice had always been, "Blood is thicker than water. Always trust family before friends." Now I'm confused. *How can you do that when your family does sinful things?*

Finally, as though Pop could read my mind, he cautioned us to never bring up the subject of the Loomis Gang anywhere. "Too many people still harbor resentment against the Loomis name. Their families experienced financial ruin because the gang terrorized all of central New York and beyond."

It's become horribly clear why children in school had hissed "horse thief" today. I will defend all of us someday if I have to.

* * *

Our first term at school ends January 1908. I'm promoted to third grade, skipping second grade entirely. Despite our last name, George and I are thriving in school and making a few friends during recess. Most of the children live on farms and have chores after school like we do. It helps to have that in common.

In September 1911, Mr. Mason becomes our teacher. He promptly assigns the Loomis children to the back row of the classroom. Pop warns us to behave because the Mason family had been most maligned by the Loomis Gang.

I'm not going to worry about anything but trying to be a good student, I decide. School is uneventful until early October when, on our pathway home, I spot an older boy, a known bully, pulling my brother Joe's hair.

I shout, "Pick on someone your own age. He's only six years old!"

He moves his freckled face close to mine and says, "Make me!"

Someone calls him Red as he pushes Joe to the ground. I scream, "Stop now, Red!"

He turns his tall, lanky body toward me, ready to make me his next victim. "Little Miss Horse Thief," he growls maliciously.

He hadn't noticed me slipping a couple rocks into my dress pocket. Catching him off guard, I trip him with my foot, sending him sprawling onto the ground.

"You will leave us alone!" I shout as I give Red the thrashing of his life. It helps to have my fists clutching rocks as I pummel him.

My parents had warned me never to start a fight, but I figure Red started this one.

"Please stop!" he begs.

"Never, ever touch my sister or brothers again!"

A small crowd of kids had gathered. Their cheers make me feel like a hero. When we reach home and report our news, Mother says, "Good for you. Protecting your sister and brothers from bullies is a good reason to fight if you absolutely must."

Since Mother's mood seems so light, I inquire, "After checking my spelling tests against my book, I know I have perfect scores. But Mr. Mason always gives me a C. Do you think he's lowering our grades because of his family's vendetta against the Loomis family?"

"Mary, my teachers were Sisters of Charity. They always taught us to pray for patience and fortitude in difficult situations."

"Doesn't it seem unfair for a teacher to lower our grades?" I press.

"We are powerless in this situation, Mary. Before bed tonight, we will begin a special prayer for our tormentors, asking that they find the love they need to feel peace, rather than abuse us."

"Thank you, Mother. That is such a good idea. It will feel good to pray, even for a teacher who doesn't like us."

* * *

When Miss White becomes our teacher in 1913, all us Loomis children improve in school. I'm taking algebra and Latin. My greatest hope is to finish high school.

Then Pop loses one of his hired workers. I'm now expected to milk our cows before dinner. On Thanksgiving, after dessert, my father begins a conversation about the increase of work on the farm with his expansion of oats and hops.

Pop turns to face me. "Mary, I need your help full-time on the farm now. You will be leaving school when you finish ninth grade in June."

My eyes sting with tears as I obediently reply, "Yes, Pop."

My dream of becoming a teacher one day is disappearing. As I walk out of the dining room at dinner's end, tears flow down my face. A veil of depression settles over me.

Summer comes too soon with my prospects turning from studying to haying and picking hops, with no hope of returning to school. Mother spends every day outdoors. She favors her large flock of chickens and goats over housework. She's especially good about keeping their stalls and nesting boxes cleaner than she keeps our house.

I'm now doing most of the cooking and baking every day, too. It's a good thing we have a small apple orchard so I can make enough pies to keep everyone satisfied. Pop favors the apples for producing hard cider.

The World War begins a few days before my fifteenth birthday. We make jam and can vegetables for winter. From dawn to dusk, I alternate between working in the fields and in the house. Even though I'm young and strong, I end each day with a numbing exhaustion.

In late September, my parents leave me in charge of the farm while they take a load of squash, pumpkins, root vegetables, jams, and eggs to market. The younger children have left for school, and I'm baking before going outside. Pop had directed the hired men to cut firewood and harvest the produce garden. When I realize I'm not hearing any activity, I venture out to find them sampling Pop's hard cider. The sorry threesome are drunk as skunks!

"What is the meaning of this drunkenness?"

Old Ed puts his head down in shame. Tom and Jimmy attempt to shock me by turning quickly with erect genitalia, like bucks in rutting season. Their intent to take advantage of me ends quickly as I pivot, grabbing a nearby ax. They run, stumbling, thinking I have castration in mind.

I loudly pronounce, "Drunken, disgusting behavior will end today!" I swing the ax into the wooden staves of each barrel. Splinters of wood fly everywhere, while the golden-brown liquid seeps into the ground. I feel like the newest member of the Woman's Christian Temperance Union.

Swinging the ax with all my strength, about to bust the last barrel, I hear Pop's voice shouting, "Girl, you don't know what you're doing!" He jumps out of the wagon and runs toward me.

"I certainly do know what I am doing," I declare.

I burst the twelfth barrel with the force of Artemis, sending debris in every direction. As I do, I pledge to stand my ground, to fight back, to not be bullied by anyone ever again.

Constance A. Dodge: Writing about Mary Loomis gave me a deeper grasp of the hardships and shame my maternal grandmother faced as a child, and, yet, she was still able to love and care for others – especially me. Her love sustained me. Our bond was very psychic, even as her life was ending at the age of 83. I'm a full-time artist and teacher. I graduated from Nazareth College, then earned an MFA from Catholic University. My art showed in NYC for twenty-three years. I now live in Edinburg, NY, where my studio is located. I'm proud to report I've never stolen a horse, pig, or muff.

An American Education
by Josephine Pasciullo

Frances Marie Alaimo Gerace (1908-2006)

This isn't the first time I've crossed the Atlantic Ocean. The trip will take several days, so I have time to think about how getting to America will help me fulfill my dream of going to school. Of getting a real education.

I first crossed a few years ago. My parents were seeking better conditions for the family than they'd had in Termini, Sicily. They and my older sister, Rose, made it as far as Bahia Blanca, Argentina, where I was born a year later, and another daughter was born a year after that.

Like many Italians, they planned to enter the United States through Argentina because of quotas limiting mass migration from southern Europe. Some Italians settled in Argentina, but others were able to use it as a doorway into the U.S.

We'd hardly settled in Bahia Blanca when my parents decided to go back to Italy. That turned out to be a bad decision because the World War had started, and Papa was conscripted immediately upon return. We were separated for the first time.

Army pay was minimal, and money was short, so Mama took a job at the grand hotel Della Termini in Termine Immerse. My parents used this time to plot how they were going to get to America when the war was over.

Mama never had the chance for a formal education herself; school was not universal or free in Italy. She had dreams, though, of her daughters becoming educated. She was determined we would be, once we were settled. She wanted us to learn more about the world than the sewing, tatting, and crocheting taught by the nuns to fill our hope chests.

My two brothers, Filippo and Antonio, were born in Sicily, and as soon as Filippo was old enough, he got to go to school. He was the first-born son, the *primo figlio*, who earned special privileges just by being born. Mama's determination to send her girls to school, too, made a strong impression on me. I adopted her dream for myself.

After the war, when quotas were relaxed because laborers were welcomed to build up America, Papa set out to seek his fortune. Like many other heads of families, he went alone to the New World. But he didn't find his fortune there, so he believed he'd be more successful back home. He notified Mama he'd be returning to Sicily.

This must not happen! Mama told herself and, in response, quickly devised a plan.

"Rosina! Francesca! Vieni qua!" Mama called from the house. The urgency in her voice told me I'd better get there immediately. Rose and I reached Mama at the same time.

"Che cosa, Ma?"

"Imballate i vestiti. Voi andate in America!" My heart sank to my stomach. I didn't want to pack up. I didn't want to move!

"Perche, Ma? Why? I want to stay here!"

Mama explained, "If I send some of the family over, Papa won't be able to come back here. You will be able to go to school for free in America."

I continued to complain loudly. "I don't want to leave you."

"We can't afford to send everyone together. I will come next year with your sister and brothers."

Nothing I said changed her decision.

With money she'd been saving for all of us to eventually join Papa, she booked passage for Rose and me, our grandmother, and a cousin to board a ship headed for the New World.

While she often deferred to Papa in small things, she won when it was important to her and, probably, without Papa realizing there'd been a contest.

* * *

Mama, my younger sister, and my brothers arrive the following year as she'd promised. Mama won't let Papa subject the family to the same life we left behind. I am going to school! School here isn't just for boys, like in Italy. Mama makes sure our clothes are in the fashion of the day so we don't look very different from our classmates. I enjoy school and the praise from my teachers. I believe I can make it to college, even though Rose dropped out of school as soon as she could. She didn't care to study like I do.

But another crisis looms.

Two more children have been born since we came to this country – two more mouths to feed. "You have to leave school at the end of the year to help support the family," Mama tells me. "Your father hasn't been able to get a job that pays enough for all of us. What Rose brings in is not enough."

I can't breathe when I hear these words. But I know I have no choice. Papa has no skills to offer in the country's current financial situation and can only get menial jobs. He's learned it's cheaper for a company to hire a child because the head of the family would want more money. His pride is wounded, but money is money.

"We will speak with the priest. He will help you get a job," my father says in an attempt to console me. He's heard that this pastor helps immigrant families negotiate the ways of the New World. Although I am only fifteen years old, the priest agrees to vouch for my being sixteen, old enough to get working papers.

Is that a lie?

My job in a woolen mill isn't glamorous, but it's one of the few places that hires immigrants. Work is exhausting because the machines run all night, and so do Rose and I. Each spinning machine spans two floors, and they continue to wind even if the yarns break. We have to run upstairs and down in order to tie the strands back together.

I know the family needs the few dollars I bring home every week, but it certainly isn't spent on meat, for that is hardly ever on our table. Our meals usually consist of Mama's delicious homemade bread and whatever vegetables are cheapest. We do love our pasta, though, the basis of every meal with whatever greens or beans we can afford.

Our situation changes again in a few years when Rose disgraces herself and our family, in spite of the fact that girls are always chaperoned. My parents are determined I am not going to end up like her.

"You have to get married!" they inform me.

"Ti prego, non ancora! Please not yet," I beg, unable to stop my tears. "I promise I won't even speak to a man if you don't make me get married now!"

I've been in this country only five years, with hardly a chance to get used to American ways before having to adjust to another change – marriage at seventeen!

My pleas get me nowhere. Tradition and the family's *face* matter, not what I want. I'm to be married as soon as they can find an eligible suitor. They consult a marriage broker who identifies a young man of whose character and history they approve.

I watch my dreams of education fly out the window. I can't change their minds now.

* * *

Gust came to America when he was nineteen, after serving in the World War. His first job was in the Pennsylvania coal mines, but he didn't want be underground the rest of his life. Some people from his village in Sicily had settled in Jamestown, so he moved here to try his luck. He worked in a bakery until he was able to get a job in a factory that paid a decent wage.

At twenty-six, he'd concluded it was time to get married and start a family. He'd consulted the same marriage broker.

Mama and Papa arrange for me to get on the trolley near our home so I can get a glimpse of my-husband-to-be, supposedly without his knowledge, before we meet at the altar. He looks kind and is not bad looking. I might do worse if I hesitate.

I nod my head *yes*. We marry on a snowy day in April 1925. In the wedding pictures, I am smothered in flowers, and no one is smiling.

After the wedding, I ask myself, *Now what, Frances Maria Alaimo Gerace?* I didn't get everything I wanted when we moved here, but I'd hoped for more formal schooling and a more comfortable life than our family had in Italy. But my dream of going to school is on hold indefinitely.

My husband and I become acquainted and grow up together as we exchange our individual goals and dreams for those we want to achieve as a family. At first, I'd worried that I'd traded one master for another because Gust was raised to rule the household. Luckily for me, he is less bound by tradition. I have a better command of English than he, and that gives me an advantage because I can communicate more easily with people outside the family.

Relatives and friends expect that children will soon follow our marriage. Gust and I agree that if we are blessed with children, they'll be able to go to school and create their own dreams. We know we'll have to work very hard; the sacrifice will be worth it. We came to *The Land of Opportunity* to fulfill our dreams for a better life for our family. Our goals are to build a nice house, start a family, earn enough to be comfortable, and become respected in the community.

I made the right choice by accepting Gust as my husband. I feel confident we will succeed.

Since my English is free of the grammatical errors many immigrants make, I am able to negotiate with the *Americani* who hold our destiny in their hands. I confide to Gust, "We must watch how educated Americans speak and get ahead. We can learn much by studying them."

* * *

"Why don't you buy the empty lot across the street from us?" friends in Lakewood suggest. "It's available through a tax sale."

"Oh, Gust, shall we? If we can save the money before it's sold to someone else, we can bid on it." Gust nods in agreement. He doesn't talk much, but I can tell when he is enthused.

The lot is out in the country on a dirt road, which is probably why it's still available. To earn the money to build that house, we have to work forty hours a week at our jobs and build in our free time. Thank goodness, I never left the mill, and Gust kept his job in the foundry.

We pay as we build because it's impossible to save ahead. We need equity or security for a loan, and the lot doesn't qualify. Banks don't easily grant loans to immigrants, especially to Italians in this community of northern European immigrants who arrived first and suspect us of wanting to take their jobs.

We don't have a telephone so I use a neighbor's line to call Green Brothers Lumber when we need building materials. Now that they know and trust us, they let us pay in installments. They are some of the good people who lend a helping hand to people like us, struggling to get ahead.

We are usually too tired to complain. Putting the siding on and adding the roof inspires us to keep going. Gust and I celebrate. "Nothing fancy, right now barely four walls, a roof, and a floor, but it's ours!" we declare.

It can be a struggle, though, to keep up our enthusiasm. A typical day goes like this: Gust works in the factory, then he works on the house. I take him dinner, then I work in the mill. We don't have a car, so we take the trolley forth and back, five miles from our apartment. It means a lot of walking to and from the trolley stops.

"It's not a grand house by any means," Gust describes it to friends. "About eight hundred square feet, including the second floor. We reach our bedroom by ladder for now."

I don't want people to think we're going to live this way forever, so I interrupt to describe our plans. "I'll sew curtains myself on a treadle machine. We're saving money for hardwood floors and a grand new hardwood staircase. When we get water and gas on the street, we'll add a furnace, and a bathroom with hot and cold running water. No more baths in a tub in the kitchen with water heated on the cast iron coal-burning stove!"

"We eat in the kitchen now, but there's space for a full dining room," Gust adds.

I have my eye on a beautiful china closet and fine china at the department store. Gust wants a living room with stuffed furniture where we can listen to the radio and relax. We'll have to discuss our priorities.

"When we have kids," he explains, "we'll build a new entrance and a music room for a piano so they can take lessons. We'll have a car of our own. We might even think about taking a vacation."

* * *

We're now residents of Lakewood and citizens of the United States. We're registered to vote. One thing I've learned: You have to participate in your community if you want to accomplish anything. I frequently quote from the Bible: "Ask and you shall receive." Quietly to myself, I add, *If you don't ask, you won't receive. It doesn't happen by wishing.*

I've become more politically active and am getting an education by being a good American citizen. I go door-to-door in the neighborhood, getting signatures requesting public services like tarred roads, electricity, public utilities, and postal delivery. Or whatever else the community lacks that government is supposed to provide with our tax money.

Our neighbors benefit from my political action but haven't caught on, yet, that in America, we don't have to accept the status quo. "Don't be afraid," I tell them. "You've got to vote and work with the politicians to get the things you need!"

We've become respected members of our community. We're confident we'll find a way for our anticipated children to go to college so they can enjoy the formal education we were denied.

I'm finally getting my education in America. Not by going to school, but by questioning what I see – observing, studying options, and, finally, by testing possibilities through trial and error. I've learned from experience and by observing how successful people become successful. They aren't afraid to ask questions; they work with community leaders. I'll never earn a formal degree, but that's not important to me anymore. I now understand what being educated really means.

Josephine Pasciullo: My mother lifted herself and her family out of poverty and into statewide recognition by sheer determination, and by revising her priorities to overcome obstacles. She inspired many others to become politically active, and writing her story has reinvigorated my activism, even though I'm nearing the age when she died at 97. Raised in western New York, I'm a former educator with a lifelong interest in politics, serving as president of the Saratoga Springs League of Women Voters and as a board member of the NYS League in the 70s. I live in Saratoga Springs, NY, where my interests include social justice, yoga, and tai chi.

Anything is Possible
by Joyce Hunt Bouyea

Elizabeth (Betty) Campbell Hunt (1913-2002)

"I thought we didn't talk about politics in polite society," I tell my mother.

"It's 1927," she responds. "Times are changing, Betty." For on this late spring afternoon, my family is walking up Tennyson Avenue in Syracuse, New York to see politics in action. Mother, Pa, my younger sister, Alice, and I want to take a look at the stoplight on the corner of Milton Avenue and Tompkins Street. I'm fourteen, and, again last night, local teenaged-boys pelted the light with rocks – *Irish confetti*, we call it – to render it useless.

"Why do they keep wrecking the stoplight?" I ask.

"They can't bear to see Britain's red over Ireland's green. That stoplight makes them furious." As Mother explains, I hear her amusement, and she adds with a smile, "You can't stop the fighting Irish."

Most people in the Tipperary Hill vicinity support the light's destruction, for Tipp Hill is Syracuse's Irish neighborhood, the area settled by immigrants fleeing poverty and persecution. We don't welcome reminders of British power.

"We're Americans," Pa declares. "England no longer rules us."

As we walk up Tennyson Avenue, we pass dozens of large two-family homes. They're well-tended, their small yards mowed, sidewalks lined with pansies. We wave at our neighbors, mostly immigrant families. Like us, they aim away from the label "shanty" Irish; we strive to be "lace-curtain."

"Some merchants aren't happy about the broken stoplight," my mother continues as we round the corner. "All the commotion disrupts business."

"Maybe we should stop for a dish of ice cream." I look toward the drugstore. "To help business."

A few minutes later, after we inspect the shattered stoplight, I sit and spin on a soda fountain stool as the soda jerk scoops up big bowls of vanilla ice cream.

"I talked to Huckle Ryan after church." The counterman sets the bowls before us. "He's got an idea for the stoplight that's as delicious as this ice cream."

Huckle is our city alderman, and we see him every Sunday at Mass at St. Patrick's. Outside church, while the grown-ups corner Huckle to voice their concerns, I check out the new shorter skirts. I see which girls have bobbed their hair. I talk with friends about the latest Charlie Chaplin moving picture. I love the changes, and, as I get older, I feel a strong draw to be more modern.

In the year that follows, Huckle's delicious idea comes to life, and, in 1928, Mother, Pa, Alice, and I once more trek up Tennyson Avenue to see what the buzz is about.

"Take a look at that!" Pa points to the new light crowning Tipp Hill. "Britain's red no longer reigns. Our shamrock is on top – where it belongs."

We gawk with friends, neighbors, and strangers from other Syracuse neighborhoods to admire the new fixture: A stoplight that reverses the traditional color order.

"Huckle convinced Crouse-Hinds to make a light with green on top," Mother tells us. "He barked like a bulldog until City Hall agreed to buy it." On St. Patrick's Day of this year, city authorities gave up. Tired of replacing costly stoplights, they accepted the solution offered by Crouse-Hinds, a Syracuse manufacturer of electric traffic signals.

Onlookers praise Huckle. "Stubborn as a towpath mule," someone says.

I love that image. In school, we've learned about towpath mules, those dogged animals that pull boats along the Erie Canal, the New York State waterway that runs through Syracuse. We're taught the quiet, lumbering mules are vital to our region's prosperity.

"I think we should celebrate," I tell my parents as we head back home. "This stoplight is special. Can we stop for ice cream?"

"Not today," says Mother.

"Please?"

She shakes her head. "No, you've had plenty of sweets all week."

She's right. We had a taffy pull party with some of our friends, and Aunt Mary's angel food cake that we had for dinner last night calls for a full cup of sugar.

"But the light's a victory for the Irish," I plead. "It's a big deal for Tipperary Hill. Right, Pa?"

Pa, who loves ice cream, checks his wallet. "You've got a point, Betty."

A few minutes later, we're back at the soda fountain. "Two scoops," I order. Before the counterman can dig into the icebox, I add, "Of chocolate."

I love change. And I can be as stubborn as a towpath mule, too.

* * *

Months later, no one has touched Huckle's green-over-red stoplight, nor have any accidents occurred. The light hangs as a reminder of what our community can accomplish. Sitting in our front parlor, Mother tells me, "You know Al Smith is the first Catholic to run for president."

"We've talked about him in school."

She sets aside her sewing, a sign that the conversation is serious. "Huckle Ryan represents us well in Syracuse. Al Smith can do the same for us in Washington. Every Catholic should be running alongside him."

I'm glad for a reason to stop doing my homework. And I'm glad Mother thinks I'm old enough to discuss adult topics. "Isn't every Catholic running with Smith?"

In 1928, the Temperance Movement is at its height. Mother and Pa enjoy their whiskey, so Smith's anti-Prohibition stance delights my parents as much as his Vatican faith. "Most Catholic men around here will probably pull the lever for Smith," Mother says. "Women may be a different story."

"Why won't women vote for Smith?"

"It's nothing to do with the candidate," she says. "Some women may not vote at all."

In 1920, the 19th Amendment to the Constitution granted women the right to vote, although in New York State, we'd won the battle three years earlier. Mother cherishes the victory, and I can't wait. In six years, at twenty-one, I'll be able to vote, too.

"When the law changed, minds didn't change as quickly," Mother explains. "Even today, many men don't believe women should vote."

"But everyone lives by the same laws," I argue. "Shouldn't everyone vote for the people who make them?"

"You'd expect so. But some women feel uncomfortable voting, thinking it's not their place. They're content to let their husbands select the leaders."

"I'll never be one of those women! How can that happen?"

"I hope it won't happen." Mother takes up her sewing again. "I'm going to campaign for Al Smith. You're welcome to come along, Betty."

Mother's decision to campaign for Governor Al Smith to be president of the United States is not a surprise. In addition to being a Catholic Democrat and part of the Progressive Movement, Smith is also Bertha Gott's father-in-law. For decades, Bertha's father worked with Pa as an engineer on the New York Central Railroad. My mother and Bertha's mother are both members of the Railroad Women's Auxiliary.

"Of course, I'll campaign with you. But do you think people will bring up Bertha and young Al's courtship? If they do, what will we say?"

I use the word *courtship* loosely, for I've heard tons of gossip about the couple. The story of the Syracuse girl, who ran off with the Governor's son shortly after meeting him, got tongues wagging all over the city. I devoured every tidbit of the relationship, for the accounts were part fairy tale and part Hollywood script.

Mother's eyebrows rise as she again takes up her sewing. "We'll stick to the facts, Betty. Bertha met the Governor's son at the State Fair four years ago. Young Al and Bertha courted for a few months. Then, they eloped. Period."

I know my parents will expect me to find a husband as I near twenty. I try to imagine when love will happen to me. I can't tell Mother, but I hope my wedding is a long way off. I want to be a teacher and, in that profession, if I get pregnant, I'd have to leave my job.

"Although Al and Bertha are both Catholic, they chose to have a civil ceremony rather than a church wedding," Mother continues. "That's not only unacceptable to most Catholics, it's considered sinful. The Governor's family was very disappointed."

We believe Matrimony – like Baptism, Penance, Communion, and Confirmation – is a sacrament. But I'm not disappointed. Rather, I'm encouraged. Governor Smith is the most famous Catholic I know. In my mind, this scandal loosens The Church's tight grip on me. I don't plan to elope. But what if I want to teach until I'm thirty? Or longer? What if I never get married, never have children? The possibilities open up.

"Do you think Al Smith will win the election?" I ask.

"Not if the Ku Klux Klan has their way." Again, Mother sets her sewing aside. "The Klan hates Catholics, and they're supporting Prohibition. They're turning Smith's fight against Hoover into a bitter one."

I've seen newspaper pictures of burning crosses and white-sheeted figures. Although I do not believe every Catholic teaching, my heart stirs with anger to think anyone hates us because of how we worship.

"When do we start campaigning?"

Times are changing, and I intend to be part of the change.

* * *

The following week, my mother and I walk Whittier Avenue, Coleridge, and Emerson – Tipperary Hill streets named to remind us of our literary legacy.

"I'm not sure how we'll be received, but we have to try," Mother warns. "We may be shunned in some of these homes."

This is our territory, I think, as we rap on lace-curtained doors. We can handle any housewife's Irish temper. As we canvass the area, some people invite us in for a cup of tea and conversation. I note how they furnish their homes, and I sniff the air to figure out what's on the stove for supper, as I listen carefully to my mother.

"With enough votes, a Catholic could lead the greatest nation on earth," she lectures. "Tipp Hill can help make history. Look what Huckle's done for us."

At a time when women are reluctant to vote, I support my mother as she tells people *how* to vote. "Think what President Al Smith would mean!" we point out.

People are polite, and we remain hopeful. But despite our best efforts, Smith loses to Hoover in a landslide. We'll never know the impact of our personal campaign, yet one individual appreciates our work.

"Look what Alice Gott gave me."

Returning home from a Railroad Auxiliary meeting, my mother holds up her wrist to show me the gift. At the meeting, the Governor's mother-in-law had presented my mother with a bracelet to thank us Campbell women for our support.

"When I'm gone, Betty," my mother tells me, "this bracelet goes to you."

I don't want to think of such a time, but the wrap-around cuff, composed of camel-bone panels painted with Japanese scenes, is like nothing I've ever seen. Over the years, Mother wears it often. She's wearing it in 1933 when I graduate Syracuse City Normal School.

"Our first family member to become a teacher," she declares. "Next thing you know, you'll be getting married."

However, in the summer of 1938, at twenty-five years of age, I am Alice's bridesmaid. We dress at home, and, as I slip into my fancy formal gown, I suspect people feel my younger sister shouldn't be beating me to the altar. I should be the one wearing white. However, I love teaching elementary school, so I cling to my freedom. I feel no urge to settle down.

Mother fusses with Alice's veil, and the camel-bone bracelet on Mother's wrist reminds me of possibilities.

Someday there *will* be a Catholic president. The thought gives me strength and inspiration. When I'm ready, I *will* get married. Anything is possible when I imagine it.

* * *

"I have bad news." Mother greets me at the door when I come home from work on a Wednesday afternoon in May 1947. "Huckle Ryan passed away."

I can't believe it. Huckle, powerful and dogged as a mule, has been a fierce force in Syracuse politics for decades. How can this be?

Mother has tears in her eyes. "I'm heartsick for Dorothy."

I'm thirty-four years old and unmarried. Huckle had married Dorothy Kelly, a dear friend and neighbor. While many friends and relatives have stopped asking when I'll find a husband, and instead write me off as an *old maid*, my friendship with Dorothy never falters. I've confided to her that while I'm happy teaching other people's children, there are days when I yearn for my own. Now, Dorothy is a widow with two school-age youngsters.

I drop my school bag and hurry across the street to see if there's anything I can do. Dorothy and I sip coffee and, as I watch her children play, distracted from the sadness in their lives, I'm sharply aware of the circle of family life.

"What a courtship you two had!" I recall how the entire community delighted when Huckle showed signs of settling down.

"On our first date, he sent a car to pick me up," Dorothy remembers. "Huckle was so funny, smart, and kind. I couldn't imagine I was the one he wanted."

"He waited until he was sure," I say. Dorothy was almost twenty years younger than Huckle, who was nearing fifty when they married.

"I can't believe he's gone." Then she asks a favor. "Would you and Alice sit Friday night with Huckle's body?"

Dorothy is following the Catholic tradition modeled by Mary Magdalene, who watched over Jesus' tomb. We know that story well from Stations of the Cross. On Saturday morning, mourners will offer condolences to the family at home. Then, we'll celebrate Huckle's Requiem Mass at St. Patrick's.

That Friday, after supper, I head to Ryan's with Alice, who agrees to leave her husband for the night. My sister and I are honored to sit with Huckle to show our respect and to allow Dorothy to get a good night's sleep. Mother sends her regards to Dorothy, while Pa bids us farewell with a poor joke: "The only way Betty will spend the night with a man is if the fellow's dead," reminding me of my parents' frustration that I've not married. I usually shrug off their disappointment, but tonight the jab stings.

Huckle's body rests in a casket in the parlor, and Alice and I settle on the sofa for the night. Eventually, we get over our unease at sharing the small space with a corpse. I lean back and, as midnight nears, my eyelids droop. Seconds later, a sound jolts me awake.

Huckle squirms. My eyes shoot open. His body lurches. It shifts.

"Mary, Mother of God!" Alice leaps up and flees out Ryan's front door, leaving me bewildered and shaking. *Is Huckle about to rise from the dead, like Jesus Christ?*

The front door flies open. Pa takes one look at Huckle and puts an end to my dramatic notion. "Rigor mortis," he pronounces.

"Sometimes the limbs move."

Mother, clutching Alice's hand, says, "I know what you're thinking, Betty. Not possible."

But –

Huckle's green-over-red stoplight was possible.

An amendment to grant women the vote was possible.

A Roman Catholic president is still possible.

Whatever I want is possible.

Maybe it takes a death for me to realize that life doesn't last forever. Huckle's stoplight altered a time-honored sequence. Perhaps the time has come for me to consider a change as well.

* * *

The following year, when some Tipp Hill peers are expecting grandchildren, I stroll into our local drugstore. I sense a man following me in the soda fountain mirror.

"Betty Campbell?" He swivels on the stool. "Remember me? Francis."

I do remember. Tall and fair-haired, Francis Hunt had attended Syracuse Central, the city's public high school. Not from Tipp Hill, Francis lived downtown in an older, rougher part of the city. Years ago, when he hung out with our friends from Cathedral High, the guys called him *Bucky*. I remember him as sort of a wise guy.

He looks me up and down and says, "If you were dressed up more, I'd take you out for dinner tonight."

I shoot back, "I live five minutes away. I can be ready in half an hour."

In no time, I'm smitten with – yet challenged by – Francis. He's thirty-five, my age, Catholic, and never married. "A true Irish bachelor," says Mother, who agrees he's good-looking.

Pa likes his ambition. "That fellow will go places," he declares. In addition to his job as a paper salesman, Francis has bought up property in Syracuse. He's helped Greek and Italian immigrants finance businesses, and he's planning to buy a home.

After a brief courtship, I walk down St. Patrick's aisle to join my groom. Eight months later, Francis and I have our first child.

My decision to marry, not dictated by The Church or convention, is a choice that springs from the intention and the timing of my heart.

I am not a rebel; I am a witness. Risk-takers surround me, and the greatest of them is my mother. In an era of transformation, she raised me to embrace change. Our spunk comes from believing in possibilities.

And from never losing sight of the pot of gold at the end of the rainbow.

Joyce Hunt Bouyea: My mother taught me to speak out, to follow my heart, and have fun doing it. Writing her story summoned her back and brought her era into clearer focus. She was overjoyed when John F. Kennedy became the first Catholic president. And she would have been thrilled to know I wore the Al Smith bracelet to an event at the Obama White House in 2015. After teaching elementary education for years, I've returned to my avocation: Writing. I live in Saratoga Springs, New York with my two daughters. The green-over-red stoplight still sits atop Tipperary Hill in Syracuse, NY.

The Boys from the Trains
by Crystal S. Hamelink

Aldy Van Meir Hood (1898-1993)

These are painful times. Our country is not recovering from the stock market crash and the Panic of 1929. Millions are struggling to find work and feed their families. Young men and boys are leaving home to search for work anywhere in America – and that's one less mouth for their families to feed. But there are few opportunities where they come from and where they're going. The lucky ones who find jobs send money back to their families.

Many hop aboard railroad freight cars and wander from town to town in their desperate search. We call them *hobos*. They call themselves *hobos*, too, as contrasted with *bums* who stay in one place and are generally not looking for work.

My husband, Roland, is a signal engineer for the New York Central Railroad. With our young daughters, Marian and Myrtle, we live in a small town near Rochester, New York, about a mile from the tracks. We are one of the lucky families with enough money to get by. Roland recently volunteered to work half time so another engineer's job could be saved. Now each of them works about thirty hours a week. At first, I was very upset. I worry about money and am very careful with our expenses. Roland reassures me we will be all right, but explains that it would be devastating for the other young engineer and his family if he lost his job. So, I will have to try harder to save enough money to cover our bills.

We just celebrated Christmas but had no money for gifts. On Christmas Eve, I secretly confiscated my daughters' dolls. The next day, the dolls reappeared under the tree, dressed in beautiful new outfits I had sewed. We did the same last Christmas. I think Marian knows it's the same doll each year but acts very excited anyway. She understands we're doing the best we can. Myrtle is still young.

One day, Roland suggests we offer food to the hobos riding the trains. "I see them every day, Aldy. They're mostly boys or young men, from fifteen through late twenties. They live on the verge of starvation, with only the clothes on their backs. Some families along the tracks offer them food or lodging, even though these families are struggling themselves. I think we should help them, too."

I'm hesitant, worried about having enough money for ourselves, let alone strangers. Then I remember the first young man I'd met from the trains. I was nineteen, working in my parents' garden bordering the railroad tracks. So many trains went by each day that I barely took notice. Until the day a train came to a grinding halt. A handsome engineer hopped off the train, walked to the garden, leaned over the fence and said, "Hi, my name is Roland. I've noticed you working in the garden and wanted to meet you."

Meeting that boy from the train changed my life. A year later, we were married.

So, I agree to this request from my concerned husband. Our income is small but steady, and I think we can help these lonely kids looking for work far from home. Each day, I make extra food for our hungry visitors. We take advantage of our large garden, and I make lots of soups and potatoes. At least once a week, we have chicken, which is the favorite meal of our guests. It's a struggle but, like a miracle, we always manage to have enough for all to eat.

Marian is ten years old now and Myrtle seven, so they both help. Marian sets extra places at the table when hungry travelers find their way to our door, and she helps me serve the food. Myrtle gets them towels and washcloths so they can wash up before eating and returning to the trains. We all listen with fascination to their stories. One boy tells us, "We had a nice home until Dad lost his job. Then we lost our home. My parents and sisters are living in our car. That's all we have. There was no room for me. I'm going to get a job and help them get an apartment so we can be a family again."

The experiences of the hobos are similar: Sad, yet hopeful. Our girls are especially touched by their stories.

Over time, these young men start telling us about something

called "safe houses" – homes in towns across the country where hobos can hop off the train and get food, perhaps some clothes or a place to sleep. Many safe houses are owned by ministers, but others belong to regular folks like us. Hobos leave notes for each other on the trains and other places. Near rail stations, they use a "hobo code" written in chalk to identify safe houses in the towns. The code is cryptic, and only hobos know how to read it.

Our visitors teach us a few of these signs: A cross at the train station with directional arrows means the safe house of a minister or a very spiritual person. The letter U, square at the bottom, means a place to sleep. (The symbol represents a bed with upright end-posts.) A rectangle with circles on the sides represents a table with dinner plates, a safe place for free meals. There are also symbols to show if a town is unfriendly towards hobos, warning them to get back on the train immediately.

They tell us our house is labeled as the safe place to eat in our town. "Directions to your safe house are chalked at the rail station, and we're grateful. Hobos riding the tracks know you're here to help." I'm surprised but agree: Yes, indeed, we are a safe house. Other people may complain about the hobos wandering through their town and resent those who give them food and shelter. I, however, am glad we can help. Our visitors are always polite and grateful for the food and the chance to rest a while.

We add the symbol for *Safe House for Food* over our front door.

In November, a young man arrives with no shoes. I'm shocked to see him limp into our house with just cardboard taped to his scruffy socks. I need to find him some shoes. Since Roland's shoes are too small, I slip out to knock on neighbors' doors while the hobo eats with the rest of the family. No success at the first two homes; the shoes are the wrong sizes. At the third house, Mr. Mane is the right size. I explain why I need a pair of his shoes. He is unwilling, saying, "Aldy, I only have two pairs of shoes and an old pair of boots, and can't afford to buy more." I tell him about the nice young man, how the snow will fly soon, and how these hobos need us all to help.

I leave with a pair of shoes.

The young man cries when gifted with them. After that, I start knocking on more doors to collect used clothing and shoes. How happy it makes our visitors when they can have clean clothes or shoes, as well as a good meal!

Our town officials, however, are not so happy. Several times, they stop by our home and ask us to stop feeding the hobos. "It gives a bad impression of the town to have these dirty young men wandering from the tracks to your house." I continue cooking while Roland tells them we will not turn away these desperate youths.

One Saturday, Roland is out of town when the mayor and another official show up at our door. The girls are curious, but I send them to another room so I can talk alone with the visitors. I know this visit will not go well. The mayor starts by complimenting my beautiful home and African violets, then gets to the heart of his request. "You must stop feeding hobos in your home," he orders. "They are dirty and smelly, and they might rob people in town. No one wants them here. If you stop feeding them, they won't get off the trains here."

I counter, "They're just homeless kids looking for work. No one in town has been harmed by any of them."

We argue for nearly an hour. Their voices grow louder and angrier as the mayor relentlessly pressures me to stop feeding the hungry boys. Laddie, our gentle collie, begins to growl, and I excuse myself to put him in the backyard. "Wish I could growl at them, too," I tell him. I'm frustrated and angry. When I return to the parlor, I hear something drop in the next room and realize the girls have been eavesdropping. But their bad manners are not my concern right now.

As the argument continues, I get an idea. I suddenly exclaim, "Enough! You win! I will stop feeding hobos in my house." The shocked mayor pauses, then grabs my hand and thanks me profusely. The screen door has barely slammed behind the beaming officials when Marian bursts in from the adjoining room, tears in her eyes. "Ma, how could you do that? Where will these hungry boys eat?"

I waste no time. "Okay, Marian. We have to clean everything out of the garage. We'll set up our table out there. I promised to never serve these hungry kids again in my house, and I always keep my promises. We'll have to feed them in the garage from now on." Which is exactly what we do for the rest of the Depression.

The town officials throw up their hands and never again bother Roland or me about this. By the time Marian leaves for college in

1939, hungry boys are no longer appearing on our doorstep. The Depression is over. The country is back to work. I feel good about the difference we made for all these kids over the years, simply by welcoming them and sharing a good meal. Or a pair of shoes.

Crystal S. Hamelink: I'm proud of my grandmother, a woman who made a positive impact on so many lives. Aldy was bright, feisty, and kind, demonstrating spirited resistance and creative problem-solving to help others during the Depression. Writing her story brought back the sights and smells of her kitchen, as well as her essence. (My mother is Marian in the story.) Throughout her ninety-five years, she inspired me to reach out to others in need. Following a career in human resources in state government, I served as assistant director of a non-profit feeding the hungry. My husband and I reside in Ballston Lake, NY. This is my first, but perhaps not my last, published story.

The Apology
by Catherine Ruggiero Lanci

Maria Pierpaoli (1924-2016)

It was Harold's fault really. He was asking for it. I warned him so many times. At first, I tried to be nice about it; I only wanted to fit in with the other third-graders. But he wouldn't stop. Every day at school, he looked me straight in the eye and insulted me.

"Go back to Italy where you belong, you Guinea WOP," Harold uttered with a smirk. "You don't belong here."

"My name is Maria. And if you don't stop calling me that awful name, I'll scratch your eyes out."

Then I did it! I curled my fingers up like a cat and dug them into his cheeks, leaving two streaks of blood. He was shocked, and so was the teacher. But not me. He'd pushed me too far.

"Maria, apologize to Harold immediately," my teacher demands. "If you don't, you'll spend the day in the cloak closet until you do."

"Never! I'll stay in there all day if I have to!" I shout. "I'll show him. I'll show all of you. You can't put me in a closet and think I'll just go away."

"Maria, you need time to think about what you've done to Harold," she declares, as she marches me to the closet.

I've never spent time shut in a closet before. The dark usually scares me, but not today. It only makes me stronger. My teacher is right about one thing: It does give me time to think. But I won't be feeling sorry for clawing Harold. I settle down on the wooden floor, rest my head on some coats, and dream about how I got here. How I got to America.

My father came over first to find us a home. After he got

everything set up for us, we'd be joining him in Cohoes, New York. He'd never met me because I was born many months after he left. He didn't even know I was on the way! Actually, my mother didn't know I was coming, either. She didn't realize she was having twins. My brother, Giulio, was born first, and then I tumbled out, still in a sack of water that the villagers called *the veil.* There's a legend that babies born this way are special. We're given divine protection and are especially sensitive to people and circumstances. This sixth sense inspires us to try to make things better for ourselves and others.

Even though I was born with *the veil,* I was so small they feared I might not live through the day. The midwife wondered if I should even be given a name. But my mother believed I was a fighter. She named me Maria, after the Blessed Virgin Mary.

I was fed my mother's milk on a small spoon, like a baby bird. But for some reason, God took my sweet brother back to heaven instead of me when we were only two days old. I was the one who lived to be strong and healthy. Momma said it was because I'm here for a reason. But I think of Giulio sometimes and wonder why God chose him and not me. I think *the veil* had something to do with it. It gave me protection and the awareness that my life mattered.

So, you see, Harold? I do have a place in the world, and I will fight to protect it. Why would I ever apologize for that?

The closet door squeaks open. "Maria, are you ready to say you're sorry to Harold?"

"No, never!" I respond.

Two years ago, my mother, my older brother, Mario, and I boarded the SS Augustus. It was a brand-new luxury liner christened by Mussolini's daughter, Edda. It had a ballroom, elegant dining rooms, and even a fancy deck for children to play on. But we never saw any of those beautiful things. We were in the part of the ship called steerage, third class. It was in the lowest section, below the deck, at the back of the ship, next to the steering equipment. It was very crowded, Italians mostly. I felt at home there: People playing cards, singing in our musical language, and the aroma of salami and provolone. Mario thought it was scary and never left Momma's side. But not me! For six days, I explored every part of the ship I was allowed to be in. My mother reminded me to be careful and make sure I knew my way back to her. They could never figure out why I had to be so busy all the time. She would call out, "Maria, sempre gira." (*You're always on the move.*)

Back in Italy, Momma had liked to stay close to home. So, I knew this trip was difficult for her. I tried turning it into an exciting adventure by making her laugh over stories about the people and things I discovered. Once I came back with an orange an old man had given me. He was charmed by the way I laughed and danced. This was a once-in-a-lifetime chance, and I wasn't going to miss out on anything. The world was opening up beyond our small village in the Italian hillside, and it was gigantic.

You see, Harold, I made a lot of friends on that ship, and I want to be your friend, too. So, why do you make it so hard for me?

The first time I saw the Statue of Liberty, I knew we were almost home. My mother told me this statue meant we were welcome; America would be a special place. I would finally get to meet my father; we would be a family. She reminded me it had been six years since she'd seen Papa. She seemed a little nervous and that made me wonder what he would think of me. Would he like me?

Upon arrival, the doctors boarded the ship to inspect the first and second-class passengers. Those of us who'd traveled in steerage went to a place called Ellis Island. The doctors had to make sure we were healthy enough to stay. Momma told us to be very quiet and do whatever was asked of us. I did my best to be brave because I knew this was a very important moment for our family. A doctor looked under my eyelids with a cold metal tool. I stood very still but was shaking on the inside. In another line, doctors were putting letters on people's jackets with white chalk. If the doctor scrawled an X on your jacket, it meant there might be something wrong with your mind, maybe you were a little crazy. I heard awful stories about sick children and feeble old people being sent back to Italy.

But not us. We were not marked with any white letters, but instead were presented with admittance papers. We were allowed to enter America!

I wasn't going back to Italy, Harold. I was good enough to stay. The doctor said so. I am not without papers!

The closet door opens again. "Maria, are you ready yet to

apologize to Harold?" I softly respond, "No." Sometimes, I'm still afraid the doctor may have made a mistake, and I will have to go back.

I'd never seen a photograph of my father, but I picked him right out of the sea of faces waiting on the dock. It's true what they said about my sixth sense: There are some things I just know. They bubble up from deep inside me.

It was our big dream, and it had finally come true, Harold. Don't you see how scary it was for me to really believe it was happening? I had to hold onto it real tight so no one could take it away. I will not let you steal my family's happiness, Harold. I belong here, too, whether you like it or not!

I'm getting hungry. I wonder if the other kids have eaten lunch yet. My friend, Eleanor Smith, always swaps with me. She thinks my salami sandwiches are unusual and delicious. She's right about that; my father does make the best salami on the block, and Momma's quite the baker. My sandwiches don't seem so special to me; they're what we always eat. I'm happy to swap because I love Eleanor's egg salad sandwiches on soft, white American bread. But it's the mayonnaise I love the most! We never have that in our house; our flavors are olive oil, vinegar, and garlic.

I see a crack of light again. "No, I won't apologize," I announce even before my teacher asks.

Thinking about food reminds me of the time our family had to move because of rotten pears. We were living in an upstairs cold-water flat owned by The Church. Father Roberts warned my parents that we children were not allowed to play near the nuns' convent or the church. That included the beautiful pear tree near the convent, which I could see from my bedroom window.

It was mid-October, and the tree was still full of fruit. I convinced my brother that the nuns wouldn't mind if we ate the fallen pears – it wouldn't actually be stealing. Slowly and quietly, we approached the tree, being careful to only take the rotten ones on the ground. We each grabbed a few and ran home. When you're hungry, even rotten pears are a treat.

That night, the priest banged on our door. He announced that we must move immediately because the nuns saw us stealing pears, and that was a sin. I couldn't believe this was happening! What had I done? How could I fix things for my family? It was so confusing that the nuns and a priest could be this mean!

I recalled my mother's words: "Maria, Dio ti ha dato una voce, usarla." (*Maria, God gave you a voice, use it.*)

I blurted out, "Father Roberts, I confess it was my idea. I never thought it could be a sin because we did not pick from the tree. We only took pears that had fallen. Father, no one else would want to eat rotten pears. Isn't it also a sin to let God's food go to waste?"

He didn't answer me, but instead spun around to address my parents. "I'm happy to be rid of you. I never liked your kind!"

I asked him what "kind" we are. His face, twisted red with hate, spat out, "Italian."

He was French, Harold. What "kind" are you?

When the priest left, my father's strap came out again. "Why can't you do what you're asked to do? Why make trouble for the family?" He was looking straight at me. I told him I was sorry, that it would never happen again. But it was too late. We were forced to leave with no place to go. The weather was starting to turn cold, making it much worse.

I must have fallen asleep because when the teacher comes in, she tells me, "Maria, it's time to go home. You have one last chance to apologize to Harold."

"I will not. I cannot. I have earned my right to be here, just as much as Harold has. I have thought about it all day, like you said, and I am not sorry. I would do it again if I have to."

I dawdle on my walk home, lingering around the pond and strolling down Myrtle Street. I'm in no rush to get there. What are my parents going to do when I tell them about my day at school? Will there be another beating, with pleas from my father to just keep my mouth shut and try to fit in?

I wonder what will happen at Harold's house when his parents see his face. Will I have to spend another day in the closet? I will if I have to, but this time I'll bring my lunch in with me.

When I tell my parents about it, my father gets mad, and I hear the same argument, just like over those stupid pears. But, to my surprise, there is no beating, and nothing more is said about it that night or ever again.

The next morning at school, Harold greets me as *Maria*. I let it sink deep into my soul. My name never sounded so sweet.

I'm sure the future will hold more chances to use my voice and just as many not to. I will be guided in knowing the difference because I was also taught, "Sta'fermi, Maria. Ascolta il tuo cuore. Ti guida sempre." (*Stand still, Maria. Listen to your heart. It will always guide you.*)

Catherine Ruggiero Lanci: Everyone has an incident that marks and changes them for life – this story is my mother's. At a young, formative age, she demonstrated defiance against injustice. She didn't tolerate it then or in her challenging 92 years of life. She modeled resilience, tempered with grace and dignity; it seemed to nourish her. I'm a lifelong resident of Saratoga Springs, NY, where my husband and I raised our five children. I enjoyed a career as a nurse, wellness educator, and a restaurateur. In retirement, I write poetry and prose.

To Joyce
Speak your Truth
Sue Van Hook

Letter Never Sent
by Sue Sweet Van Hook

Dorothy Elizabeth Van Twisk Sweet (1914-1999)

Dear Mother,
I am not certain where to begin, but begin I must. I am very upset by your latest letter and must let you know my true feelings.

You assault my capabilities when you question whether I can get the new apartment ready. You accuse me of judging your help as unsatisfactory, even before you offer it. And then you tell me about all the people you are writing letters to, including my fiancé and his mother, without letting me know the content! Apparently, you believe I'm negligent in getting thank-you letters in the mail. I feel insulted by this.

The worst part is that twice you tell me to be thoughtful of Dick. "He is so good," you write. You cannot issue a written directive to convince me to be good to Dick. How else would I treat the man I am to marry? The man you are forcing me to marry.

For too long, I've succumbed to your directives. I understand and appreciate your concern for my future welfare, given your tenuous hold on life. But it is my life you are deciding, causing me to feel pressured and confused.

I thought you sent me to college to pursue a career after graduation, to become financially independent, to make the world a better place. Mormor and Farfar were so fortunate to have left Sweden in 1872, escaping the potato famine to start a better life here. I want a better life, too. I want to be successful like your two older sisters who worked as brokerage clerks for that big firm in Manhattan. I want to work outside the home.

I am well aware of the privilege you bestowed on me to send me to St. Lawrence University, the first in our family to continue education beyond high school. I took that opportunity so very seriously. I didn't just succeed; I excelled! It wasn't easy. The winters in Canton were long and cold. We were still wearing our full-length wool coats in April.

Away at school, I missed home. I longed for kitchen conversations with Mormor, and I craved Uncle's taunting attention. But nothing compared to the grief I felt when Aunt Hulda ended her life after the stock market crash. Perhaps you do not know how much I miss her. I set out to work with numbers because of her and Aunt Sadie.

To escape the nagging ache in my heart, I overloaded myself with classes, athletics, and extracurricular activities. You may remember, Mother, that I was inducted into Kalon, the highest honor for a scholar athlete. I was also a member of the Saint Lawrence University Club, which honors athlete scholars. I still laugh at the thought of the two organizations – the former emphasizing academic achievement over sports; the latter, the reverse. But, in reality, the same women are in both. Field hockey, basketball, speedball, tennis, volleyball, and canoe racing – I played them all. I won the canoe-bobbing race up the Grass River through campus. What a thrill it was to straddle the stern gunwales and propel the canoe forward with deep-knee bends and upward thrusts! At 5'11, I had extra length in my legs that gave me more leverage against the fulcrum point of the canoe. You know how much I love being on the water with Dad, fishing in Long Island Sound or sailing his catboat. I feel so free and easy, buoyed up by waves and wind. Something I don't feel most of the time due to the pressure you place on me.

I tried as many activities as I could manage while away at school. I joined the Glee Club to sing as we did around the piano at home. I played popular tunes to console myself – *Am I Blue?* was a favorite, reflecting my mood much of the time. The Mummers Drama Club was fun for a short while, but managing the Women's Debate Team really bolstered my self-confidence. I always thought of Aunt Hulda and Aunt Sadie before going onto the debate stage. When I prepared to think clearly and keep track of my arguments, I imagined the two of them bearing responsibility for accurate calculations. Their courage and determination as Wall Street women helped shape me. They both chose careers over raising a family.

Instead, you had Richard and me. It wasn't hard for me to figure out that you were two months pregnant with me when you married Daddy on Christmas Eve. Did the pregnancy rob you of a career, I wonder? Was I an unwanted child? I always felt like one.

After graduation, I left my job teaching high school in Dannemora after one year to take a position at Wappinger's Falls High School. I did this to be nearer to you and Dad, Richard, and our Brooklyn family. And you are now asking me to give up this job to be married?

I've often asked myself why you rule our household. Dad is easy to talk to, but seems to always defer to your decisions. That was true even before your diagnosis. He earns the wages for us all, so shouldn't he be in charge? Richard keeps to himself, always tinkering. I suppose it's his way of steering clear of you much of the time. He has found his love in Geraldine, and I am happy they see one another so often.

Me? I've never found my voice in your presence. Isn't it ironic that I am an acknowledged debater but have not been able to debate you, Mother?

Perhaps it is your Christian Science faith that elevates you to a place of power in our home. Your ability to heal your own wounds and those of others in the community have astonished us all. Your hands have the golden touch. I remember the time you accidentally dropped the hot iron on your forearm. You asked us to leave the room so you could pray. When you emerged, your arm was red, but the skin was intact. At that young age, I believed you could perform magic. So, you can understand why it has not made sense to me that you could die from this disease.

At first, I was devastated by the news of your tuberculosis. It was hard to be away at college, not knowing how you were doing day by day. I did not understand why your life should be taken so early. I told myself you would not die: *Mother is stoic.* As the months wore on, Dad told me the family doctor always left shaking his head in amazement that you were still alive. Four years have come and gone, and you live on.

You tell me not to worry. You trust God will heal you as He has many times before. I have witnessed your healing powers, and I want to believe you will recover. Your courage and strong faith show me the healing power of belief. Your battle with TB has given me more reason to live my life to the fullest.

None of us know how much longer we have on God's good earth. I am sorry your life is fragile in this prolonged, weakened state. But I must focus on living my life now. I love teaching high school! I am a strong, accomplished young woman who can do anything I set my mind to. Isn't that what my first-grade teacher told me weeks before the end of the school year? More than any other voice, it is hers I believe and trust. I want to teach. I want to share my love for inquiry, my passion for mathematics and the French language. I want to spend time outdoors. I want to continue to debate and win. I want to become a chess master, sing in the church choir, play the piano, and sew clothes. And I want to marry someone I look up to, someone I am attracted to, joining a heart that beats to the same rhythm as mine.

Maybe I should have taken up with a man or two during my college years; I had crushes on several. They liked me, too. Peter Vanderwater was my favorite companion. We met because of the alphabet – Vanderwater and Van Twisk always lined up together. Tall, blonde, and handsome, he was dashing. Bob and I got to know one another in the canoe regatta. He often commented on my canoe-bobbing skills but probably was more interested in my chest-heaving as I pumped the gunwales. But I didn't have much time for men, other than flirting. What time I had was spent with my sorority sisters.

When the chemistry teacher at Wappinger's Falls High School starting showing an interest in me, I was flattered but did not take our dates seriously. Apparently, you and he did. It felt as though he came to the house for Sunday dinners to visit you, Mother. It was you who grew fond of Dick, not me. But to promise my hand in marriage to him without consulting me first – what were you thinking? Why would you accept a marriage proposal on his behalf and not mine?

Do you realize, Mother, that you are forcing me to choose between a career and marriage? Married women do not get hired as teachers. Look at the sacrifices your sisters made to remain in their jobs – no children! A few years ago, Congress passed the Federal Economy Act to limit government employment to the household head, typically a man. The federal government is trying to keep women in the home to care for the family! That's not fair. I have a college degree!

You are living on borrowed time, and it seems your ultimate goal is to see me and brother Richard both "happily" married before you leave us. Is this the reason? If so, I will try to understand your wishes for me.

I chose to go to college to have a career, and I'm off to a good start. If I must marry now to please you, I know that someday I will make a difference in the lives of students so they remember my words, as I have treasured those of my first-grade teacher. I will do this in spite of the marriage thrust upon me. I will make that work, too. I will find ways to love this man you adore, to bear his children, to cook his meals, and do his laundry. I will make him laugh and learn to accept the things I cherish. I will give in to this union with hope for a loving future. I do this for you, Mother, so that you may die in peace.

Your dutiful daughter,
Dorothy

Sue Sweet Van Hook: My mother's first-grade teacher had told her she could do anything she put her mind to; it was the most important lesson of her life. Dorothy resumed her own teaching career after twenty years of raising children and suffering the loss of a 13-year-old son. She was a strong woman of faith. Our relationship was one of respect, but lacked affection. I wrote this story to embody my appreciation and love for her. I'm a mycologist, naturalist, teacher, and healer. I believe maintaining a connection to the earth is essential for well-being. After careers in land conservation, biology, and applied mycology, I retired to write in Cambridge, NY.

Annie's Rings
by Cathy Fedoruk

Annie Slupska (1913-1984)

"Ne rukhaysya, Mama. Don't move," I instruct, as I insert the needle into her fleshy upper arm. This is my morning routine. Mama needs her insulin before the first meal of the day. Every morning and evening, I must boil water to sterilize Mama's syringes, too.

Diabetes is a curse. Mama says it's God's punishment. Why her? She rubs her arm and pulls down her crumpled cotton sleeve in the same breath. She pays for the sins of Tato, and he washes his sins away with liquor. Our priest, Batko Semczuk, says, "God has a plan, and we must endure our lot in life in order to reach everlasting life in Heaven." Who wants an everlasting life like this? Here I am at twenty-six years old, living at home and caring for my parents.

"Oh, my God!" Mama curses. "Clumsy girl!"

But what would they do without me?

Mama doesn't feel well today and is in one of her moods. This is what happens when she is inconsistent with her insulin.

Today, she pays the price for skipping last night's injection. She insisted I go to bed when she realized it was one of Tato's impossible drunken nights. And to top it off, Tato gave away half the whiskey supply, a common occurrence when he drinks in excess. Tato believes men need their medicine, too. The railway workers put in long hours and sometimes can't get to the pub, so Tato helps them out.

"What are you looking at, woman?" Tato shuffles into the kitchen.

Tato was twenty-four years old when he left his family in Galicia.

His father had saved an ad from their local paper announcing free land in Canada. With never-ending poverty, and Tato making trouble in Franz Joseph I's Austro-Hungarian army, Tato's father insisted he leave their village to create a new life.

Tato claimed 160 acres in Canada, but all he could afford was a ticket in steerage to get there. He crossed the Atlantic on the Lake Erie Steam Ship in March 1903. It took almost two weeks from Liverpool, England to St. John, New Brunswick. To this day, Tato says he will never set foot on a boat as long as he lives.

Mama landed in Winnipeg two months after he did. They were from the same village, Peremelo, and attended the same church. Their marriage had been arranged prior to Tato's departure; they've been married thirty-five years.

Farming is in our ancestors' blood; we come from the "bread basket" of Galicia. Tato and Mama worked relentlessly and soon had a surplus of feed. And so, they started a feed business. By 1915, they'd built the store on McPhillips Street. It was the first grocery store in the North End. Now it is the place to shop. We carry everything including coffee, milk, eggs, cigarettes, canned goods, and chocolate. We also offer store credit if needed.

"I'm looking at a fool," Mama answers.

Tato opens the cabinet, takes a shot glass and his whiskey bottle, and slumps down in the chair at the end of the square wooden table. My brother's garden is in plain sight from our kitchen window. The nuthatch and chickadees visit the sunflowers on the Prichard Street side of his garden, pecking away at the seeds, while Tato's cigarette dangles from his mouth. He wheezes and inhales smoke all in the same breath. I prepare the morning coffee.

"Nothing like the hair of the dog," he coughs out, clanking down his glass. Mama's worn, chapped hands grip the table's edge as she pushes her thick body up off the chair. She avoids his puffy eyes, brushing past him. She heads back to their bedroom to rest before breakfast, sighing, "God is looking for those who come to him."

My mind drifts to Mikael. He's invited me to the moving-picture show. It's one of my favorite things to do. *The Wizard of Oz* will play downtown in a few weeks. Posters are up in the theatre. *Technicolor!* Just like my brother's blooming garden of poppies and sweet peas on a clear day. Indeed, with my Mikael, I have something to look forward to. I will definitely wear that baby blue cardigan I wore for the church carnival; it goes with my blue eyes.

"Get breakfast on, girlie," Tato shouts.

"Tato, I am going. I am going," I reply, exasperated.

I place the insulin in the icebox and the hypodermic needle into the small aluminum pot next to the stove. I grab the worn wicker basket from the pantry. Immediately, the morning air cleanses my lungs of the smoky, rancid kitchen air as I step out into the back yard. I head toward the chicken coop and, as I am about to cross Prichard, a black Ford speeds by churning up a cloud of dust, forcing me to wince. We haven't had a drop of rain for weeks. I blink my eyes to cleanse them of the dust.

"Who's that lovely lady up on the church hall wall?" Mikael had asked when we first spoke. His eyes twinkle when he speaks to me. We've been going to the same church since we were in grade school, and we've had eyes for one another for almost a year now. Attending mass at Saint Pokrova Church is the highlight of my week.

I grab my skirt so it doesn't catch on the broken, wooden doorframe. I hold my breath – it smells like chicken coop in here. The hens lay a lot of eggs, fifteen just today. There is a restlessness in the air, a sure sign of inclement weather. I move quickly, filling my basket. The anticipation of Tato's impatience makes me hurry back. A cloud formation is coming in from the east, billowing grey and white puffs. Rain will make my life easier the next few days. The accumulation of dry prairie dust throughout our house and store will be much less with a good downpour.

Tato hasn't moved from the table; he leans back, forcing his stained, buttoned shirt to stretch open. He rubs his big, bloated belly in anticipation of the meal to come and pounds his fists on the table. The *hair of the dog* is successful; his whiskey bottle is almost empty.

The frying pan is sufficiently greased from last night's potato pancakes, so I strike a match to preheat the pan. My stomach gurgles as I sip my lukewarm coffee. Tato reaches up to the radio sitting on the shelf above the table and turns the knob. The weather reporter calls for a rainstorm.

"Ochevydno! It doesn't take a genius," I blurt out.

From the kitchen window, I see my brother's wife in the garden, bent over the tomato plants. Best she get the ripe ones before the rain. Tomatoes are delicious in cabbage soup; Mama can use them in her next batch. Mikael loves cabbage soup. At the last church carnival, he had seconds.

I wonder what he is doing this morning. Likely on his way to his father's shop. It makes my heart sing to think of him. The pan spits it's ready for the eggs.

British Prime Minister Chamberlain booms from above our table, "This country is at war with Germany...Hitler uses force to get what he wants..."

The pan spatters as I crack six eggs into it. Tato's right hand is on his whiskey bottle, and his left holds a cigarette. Hopefully, he won't go into one of his rants: *The Austrians, the Russians, the Germans, they all like their war. You can't trust the damn government. Take matters into your own hands. This is what real men do.* His rage can be endless.

"German bastards causing trouble again," Tato coughs, as he squishes out his cigarette in the overflowing ashtray in the middle of the table. The eggs are almost done, and I call out to Mama. I hope breakfast will make her feel better.

"Why are you yelling? I hear you," Mama responds.

I place the leftover bread from last night on our plates. It's not fresh, but it will do the job of sucking up the sweet, runny yoke of the fresh eggs. *Eyes wide open* is how we like them. Tato grunts and wipes his mouth with the back of his big burly hand to clean the yoke that drips down his lower lip. We eat in silence with the radio. A Maxwell House Coffee tune crackles over our heads, and our forks scratch at the jiggling eggs on the Hudson Bay Company plates that Mama purchased over a decade ago.

* * *

"Bo Tyoye ye Tsarstvo, i syla, i slava, Naviky. Amin." (*For thine is the kingdom, the power, and the glory, forever and ever. Amen.*) The entire congregation, mostly women and older men, prays.

Prayer brings me peace. It makes me feel like Mikael is present. I want to believe he'll walk through the door any minute. He reported for duty more than six months ago. Last week, his father brought the news. I could see it in his gait. The sun had set, and his silhouette trudged through our backyard.

He could barely say the words. He whispered, "Mikael is gone." It happened in France; there was nothing to be done. I was in disbelief and could only get "Ni" out of my mouth. Nothing else. I froze like a statue, like the one of Mary up on the altar, above Batko Semczuk's head.

Mikael's father wouldn't stay. Wouldn't even step inside the door. I was left alone with the boiling water on the stove.

I look at the ring – the ring Mikael had given me. It was the best Christmas present. It's still on my ring finger. Batko Semczuk blesses the wine, and we kneel. I don't deserve this misfortune: I attend church every Sunday. I am a good Catholic. I care for my family. I am a devoted daughter. *Bozhe mylly, dear God, what else could I have done?*

I wonder if Mikael received my last package. Chocolate and cigarettes were what the men wanted. I also enclosed a letter with a photo of me, similar to the one he always loved in the church hall.

Annie Slupska, the grocer's daughter. What is to become of me now?

I receive the body and blood of Christ and, somehow, find myself in the hall next to my photograph. Everyone is gathering around Mikael's mother down at the other end. Her face is red, covered with tears. I glance up at my photograph. Everything about me is smiling: My eyes, my mouth, even my hair. *Blyskuchi (Sparkly) Slupska* is what he called me.

Gone forever. Stripped away in an instant. He was one of the first to enlist. It was the right thing to do. He's considered a hero.

I can't bear to be around anyone, even my best friend. I move towards the exit, and I walk. I walk without any destination in mind. I move as though in a dream. Everything is in slow motion. I drift by the school, Mikael's family's hardware shop, and our grocery store. I have passed through our neighborhood countless times with him. Perhaps I will wake up; perhaps this is a nightmare.

I find myself under a poplar tree, three doors down from his house. The broad, green leaves provide me with shade, although I am soaked in sweat. I am numb, and breathing is difficult.

War. War for liberty. Tato and Mama immigrated to Canada for a better life. What better life? There is no escaping the horrors of war. An ocean can't protect us.

My body can't cope with the heat, and I pass out.

A cool leaf lands on my cheek and awakens me. *Oy-yoy!* What happened? Where am I? What time is it? The sun is setting. I must get home. It's time for Mama's medicine. I hurry towards home and see clouds rolling in from the west. I enter through the backyard and open the kitchen door. Tato is at his spot at the table with his whiskey bottle. Mama is nowhere in sight.

"Annie, is that you?"

"Yes, Mama. I'm home."

"Where you been, girlie?" Tato grunts.

"Nowhere, Tato."

I move to the sink to fill the pot with water and strike a match to light the burner. The house reeks of chicken. I open the covered pot on the back burner. It's soup, but I'm not hungry. I am thirsty, though. My mouth is dry. I fill a glass with water and drink standing over the sink. I reach up and grab a shot glass. I sit next to Tato, placing my glass next to his. He pours for both of us.

"Dai bozhe." (*God, give us good health.*)

We clink and take our shots all in one gulp. The whiskey burns going down, but it's a soothing, numbing burn. Tato lights another cigarette. We sit in silence, waiting for the water to boil.

"Mama, come. It's time."

I rise to the stove. She shuffles to the kitchen. She has changed from her church dress into her everyday dress. She looks directly into my eyes to hug me in a sort of way that is unfamiliar and reserved for rare occasions. Not a word is uttered to comfort me. It's not our way.

Mama sits in her spot, and I insert the needle into the insulin vial and then into her arm. I can't bear the silence. I place all the diabetic paraphernalia in the sink. I grab the matches and a cigarette from the table.

The night air is crisp. I strike the match and light up. I take a drag and hold the smoke deep down in the barracks of my lungs, exhaling slowly. My cigarette smoke disappears into the air, and I wish I could, too. The moon is visible, and a few stars are revealing themselves in the openings between the clouds. I spin the ring.

I promise myself I will never marry. No one can replace my Mikael. Tears roll down my cheeks, the same cheeks Mikael held in his hands when he kissed me goodbye. "Don't worry, Annie. I will be back soon. God will watch over us."

I wish God could reach a hand into my heart and give it to Mikael now.

"Girlie, what are you doing out there?" Tato shouts.

I quickly wipe my tears, put out my cigarette, flick the butt, and smooth out my skirt as I rise off the back stoop. Tato's had a few more shots by now, and a neighbor is at the front door. Mama isn't in sight. Tato turns on the radio, and Judy Garland croons *Somewhere Over the Rainbow*.

* * *

On May 24th, 1945, only months before World War II ends, I marry Anthony Fedoruk from the North End of Winnipeg. He is a World War II veteran who bravely served Canada. I am thirty-three, considered an old maid, lucky to have found a man to marry. We have three sons together. Our eldest, John, marries Arlene, and they have two daughters. When I am sixty-nine years old, I present each of my granddaughters with an engagement ring. "Why are there two rings, Baba?" they ask. I tell them I was engaged twice. They look at me puzzled and ask which one is from Grandpa. I smile and gesture with my hands, as if to push them away. As if to say, I don't remember.

Cathy Fedoruk: My grandmother may have been born and raised in the Canadian prairies, but the Ukrainian ghetto where she spent her life was little different from the Galician village of her ancestors. Baba had a kind toughness that I loved. But when she revealed two engagement rings, noting that Grandpa wasn't her first fiancé, I knew this was the hidden source of the sadness I'd always sensed within her. After a 17-year career in the fashion industry, I graduated with a BA in creative writing and literature from NYU, and reside in NYC with my husband, two sons, and a rescue beagle.

The Girl Who Would Bring Back the Tsar
by Nadia Ghent

Natasha Ghent (1933-2006)

At night, I dream of strawberries. Sweet red berries with cream, thick and rich, juice that runs down my chin and stains the collar of my dress. The taste of strawberries fills my mouth, and in my dreams, I am eating. There are more, always more strawberries warm from the sun and fragrant in the market basket. Mama's *pannier* filled with so many strawberries, it is a bouquet of red, like poppies, like roses. There is butter also in the *pannier*, butter to eat in pieces I gouge with my thumb. Soft yielding yellow that tastes of pastures and cows and sun.

In my dreams, I am drinking warm milk in Mama's kitchen, and my tongue finds the crack in the lip of the bowl as I drink, the bowl heavy and warm between my hands. Then there is the white tablecloth, starched and stiff, and Mama sitting across from me, smoking. She stirs her tea. In the next room, the piano, the *samovar*, the bookshelf. Our cat, Blitz, asleep on the sofa. I am dreaming that Mama loves me. I dream of what I long for, and just before I wake up, when my limbs are too heavy to move, when it is still dark and cold, before I know where I am, everything vanishes. The rooster crows.

I am on the hard, stone floor of the barn that smells of straw and manure. We have left home, we are hiding, we are hungry. Mama sleeps on the floor next to me. Next to her, my violin in its black case.

* * *

Paris wasn't safe for children. The war had already started.

Some children left for the countryside before bombs began to drop from the sky. Some children with yellow stars went elsewhere on trains. Papa was in America, waiting for us. He would send tickets soon. Every day, there was the sound of police sirens. There was nothing to eat. We left Paris when the shops closed, and the streets were empty, and the wind came through the broken glass of our living room window that looked out over Boulevard Garibaldi. German soldiers were on the way. I was frightened, but secretly, I wanted to see what the soldiers looked like, if they all had black mustaches like the Führer's.

It was summer, early June. Flowers were blooming in the Jardin Luxembourg. We took the clothes we wore and my violin. Mama brought the music books, the études and concertos. Everything else was left behind.

I poured a last bowl of cream for Blitz. Mama took my hand and pulled me away. "Come, Natasha," she said. There was no time to say goodbye to Madame Perrin next door and her chow with its purple tongue. Even to linger in the hallway while the truck waited downstairs was to risk its leaving without us.

* * *

We are Russian, not French. We are a family, but we don't live in the same place. I am only seven, but I play the violin. Mama is a nurse at the clinic around the corner, and Papa lives in America. I don't know how to read, but Papa will teach me English when we see him in New York. I don't go to school because I have to practice violin all day. I would like to go to school with the other children in the neighborhood, but the violin requires many hours of practice, and Mama says I must be careful with my hands. When Mama comes home from work, she sits at the piano and tests my note-naming while I close my eyes and listen, the vibrations like whispers of sound in my ear. Notes are colors to me; I can see what I hear: Blue, magenta, ruby, cerise. Then there are two hours of études and an hour of solfège. I don't play with dolls.

Actually, Mama is not really a nurse. "We were very rich in St. Petersburg," she tells me. "There was a maid to dress me every day and many servants." Wealthy girls did nothing with their hands except for piano lessons and embroidery, she says. Now she sweeps the office floor for the doctor around the corner, rolls up bandages.

When I am sick, she lets my blood.

"This is how the doctor cured me when I was a girl," she says, "The bad blood has to be let out."

"Yes, Mama," I answer. I know what she will say next.

"You are bad, Natasha. You are *une enfant illégitime*," she says in French as she applies the leeches, as if I would not understand the words. After she fled from St. Petersburg to Paris, she was a cancan dancer in the Folies Bergère. Papa slipped a fifty-franc note under her garter and, soon after, I was born. Now, at night, she stays home while I practice. She is still proud of her slim waist, her long legs.

Papa sends us money from America.

* * *

There are twelve children and Mama on this farm in the countryside outside Paris. Mama was allowed to come with us because she told them she knows how to tend to sick children. But I know she has come to make sure I practice. The wife of the farmer does not like us. She feeds us turnips and once a week, bread. There are chickens and a rooster that scratches in the dirt for worms. The farmer and his wife will eat the eggs. The chickens will be roasted for the German soldiers who march through here on their way to Paris. Then they will leave us alone. The other children cry for their mothers and are often sick. Mama finds leeches and mixes mud into the mustard plasters she uses to make them better.

During the day, there is always the practicing to do. My violin is a quarter-size, just right for my fingers to fly up and down the fingerboard. Scales, arpeggios, Bach, then Mozart. I practice in a hayloft where I can watch the sunlight spread over the fields in the distance. I like having something to keep me occupied instead of crying like the lonely children. But I don't like to practice. Mama sits with me and directs my repetitions after she has finished with the sick ones. In French, the word *répetez* means "to practice." We repeat.

"Music feeds the soul," Mama says. But there is always work to be done even though we have so little to eat. Scales begin every morning: *Croissant*, G major. *Pain au chocolat*, D major. *Baguette*, A major. *Isle Flottante*, E major. *Camembert*, B major. *Éclair*, F sharp major. *Croquembouche*, C sharp major. Again, with the flat keys, around the circle of fifths, then the minor mode. Scale practice is endless and perpetual. *Begin again.* There is no metronome, so Mama beats time with her hands. Slow, fast, then much faster. Each key reminds me of what we don't have.

* * *

When I was four, Mama brought me to play for Monsieur Galamian at the Conservatoire Russe de Paris. I wore a blue dress and had a velvet bow in my hair. I performed a Mozart concerto by memory, and when I finished, Galamian gave me a piece of chocolate.

"I want her to be a great artist," Mama told him. Even then, I knew how desperate she was. I remember the pattern of red and gold flowers woven into the rug where I stood, listening while they talked about me, my violin tucked under my arm. "The money she makes touring around the world will be enough to bring the Tsar and his family back from hiding, and he will return to the throne of the imperial Russian monarchy. Order and civility will be restored," she told him. Mama was sure the Tsar still lived.

"Madame," Galamian replied in Russian to my mother, "she has talent, but if it's money you're after, train your cat to be a violinist. Now that would bring Tsar Nicholas back from the dead!" Then he laughed. Nevertheless, he agreed to teach me once a week.

I never liked to practice, but I loved the feeling of the tiny violin in my arms, the curves in the wood and the smell of varnish, the elegant scroll. The taut horsehair bow enclosed in my right hand. How the violin fit just right against my neck like an embrace. Like a doll that was mine, that I could always hug. The way the sound vibrated through my body, and my fingers so strong and fast. I wanted to play for Papa, but he was too far away.

I was the girl who would bring back the Tsar.

But every day, my mother loved me less as I grew older, less a prodigy and more just a growing girl. Because of the war, there could not be a debut for me in Paris. When we spoke French, she called me *mon petit chou,* but she didn't mean it in a nice way. She really meant my little cabbage – common, plain, not lovely. "You must keep practicing," Mama always said. "Someday, you will be famous and make us a lot of money." Sometimes, when she was not at home, I would listen to the radio instead.

* * *

We stay on the farm as the weather turns cold and leaves fall from the trees. My fingers are stiff in the morning as I practice. I have learned three new concertos. Sometimes, the children sneak into the barn to listen to my practicing, but Mama shoos them away. I would like to play with them, but they don't want to come too close to me or to my mother who torments them with her leeches, her blood-letting. They call her *la sorcière*, the witch, with her dark hair, her long bony fingers. She rarely smiles and is always smoking.

It grows colder, and Mama and I sleep curled together on the stone floor of the barn. There is frost on the fields, so we tie rags around our shoes because we have no boots. The chickens were slaughtered long ago; the rooster went into stew for the farmer and his wife. It is hard to practice when I am so hungry. Mama is very thin. Some days, I do not open the violin case once.

One day, the farmer's wife brings a letter for Mama. It is a thin, blue envelope from Papa, fragile like the wing of a bird. The farmer's wife has already read it. She takes it from her apron pocket and thrusts it in Mama's face. "Who will take care of the children now?" she demands. Mama and I will leave the next day at dawn in a convoy of supply trucks headed for Paris. There will be tickets waiting for us at the Cunard office on the rue de Lourmel, passage to New York, Papa writes, arranged by the Red Cross. An entire ship of mothers and children will be leaving France to join their husbands and fathers in America. "*A humanitarian gesture,*" Mama reads from his letter. "*Dearest Marie and Natasha, Bon voyage and see you soon! Papa.*"

* * *

Blitz is gone. Madame Perrin and her chow with its purple tongue are gone. There is nothing left in our apartment when we return to Paris. The furniture, the books, the silverware, Mama's *samovar*, our winter clothing, all gone. I walk through the empty rooms carrying my violin case, trying to remember what had once been there. Now only quiet, dusty wooden floors. When I practice, the sound echoes against bare walls. Soon, Mama and I will be gone, too.

* * *

My throat hurts. I can't swallow. Mama holds her hand to my forehead and takes my pulse. She brings me to the doctor's office around the corner. He is still in the office with the red cross in the window, tending to his patients by himself. He is happy to see Mama again, all the years she worked for him. "Welcome home," he says. "We have all suffered so much. I hear you are leaving again soon. Good for you."

But he is not at all happy to see me, now that I am a patient. After he listens to my heart and checks my throat, he looks at me in a serious way. I am sick, he says, very sick, and he has no medicine for me. "No leeches or mustard plasters either, Marie," he warns my mother. "This requires something much more modern. Sick children are not allowed into America." I almost cry with relief when I hear *no leeches*, but there are no tears. I can't cry. I want to go to America, but I am too hot.

"You must take her to Lisbon right away. My colleague has some medicine that he keeps just for children," the doctor says. A drug for wounded soldiers, something very new, but there is none in Paris or in the rest of France, he explains. He writes the name of this medicine on a piece of paper and on the back, directions. Another doctor will have a drug that is not leeches or mud or cold baths or my mother's hand against my forehead. I think I am dreaming, the words sound so far away.

"There will be one last ship to America in a month," he says. "You still have time."

* * *

In Lisbon, we must wait until I get better. Here, there are cream white buildings with red-tiled roofs and, from a distance, the smell of ocean in the air. Where people speak fast beautiful words I don't understand. At the doctor's house behind the clinic, there are orange trees and open windows, sunlight and gauzy curtains streaming in the warm wind that blows through every afternoon. I lie in bed, and a nurse in a white dress and starched cap, a real nurse, brings me medicine twice a day and once at night. *Penicilina,* she calls it, the thick bitter liquid she pours and spoons into my mouth. She brings me trays of food and sits with me while I eat. There are plates of fish and meat, eggs, cheese, and rice, bread with butter, milk. I eat, and I am always hungry.

My violin sits in its case, silent. Mama is not in the room with me, and I am happy not to practice. In the afternoons, another nurse reads books to me in Portuguese. I want to know what the letters mean, what the stories are all about. But the words are music I do not know. The nurse holds me close as she reads to me. One day she brings me strawberries, fat and red, and I dream of home.

Days pass in this room that smells of the sea, and I watch shadows lengthening across the walls in the afternoons. Soon I am stronger. I can walk to the window and look out over the rooftops of the city. Another day, the nurse and I stroll in the garden outside the doctor's house. There are roses blooming and flowering bushes: Jasmine, lavender, oleander, sage. On a bench in the shade, I see Mama, smoking. "You look better now," she says, but she does not embrace me. She does not smile. "Please brush your hair," she says. "And then it's time for you to practice."

When we leave, the doctor and both nurses see us off. The afternoon nurse gives me a book with golden-edged pages. A book that is only mine, but I can't read it. I want her to read it to me, but there is no time. I hug the doctor, the nurses. I hold my book close. Mama takes my hand and, in her other hand, she carries my violin case.

At the harbor, there is a Red Cross ship for refugees, the last one. As we cross the Atlantic, children cry and mothers weep. The war continues, but U-boats let us pass. Our ship rocks over the waves while I practice. Mama beats time with her hands, and I play fast, spooling out notes in long ribbons of sound, my fingers racing up and down the fingerboard. At night, I play for the captain and his crew, and sometimes they fall asleep while I play. "You are adorable," they say, but I am not as young as they think. I don't like being on display, like a cat that plays the violin. Mama listens in the shadows. She tells me later what was wrong, what must be better. I don't care. I won't always have to do what Mama says. Her dreams are not the same as mine. I dream that someday I will have daughters of my own, and I will love them all the time.

When we arrive in New York, I will beg Papa to send me to school. I want to learn what children study: Math, history, science, reading, writing. A classroom filled with busy students, and I will be among them. A pencil in my hand, blank paper. I want to read books all by myself, and I will learn the music of those words.

I can't bring back the Tsar. I know he is already dead. The violin will be my life, but it won't be my only friend. I hold the violin nestled against my body, like embracing a needy child.

Nadia Ghent: So much of my story is intertwined with Natasha's; I sometimes think I know her stories better than my own. She repeated them to me endlessly, often when brushing and braiding my hair, as a way to lessen the trauma of the deprivations she suffered. She was never able to forgive her mother, my grandmother. Writing about my mother is my attempt to lessen the impact of her loss. I studied literature at Brown University and violin performance at Manhattan School of Music. My work has appeared in *Assay: A Journal of Nonfiction Studies, Necessary Fiction*, and *Listen to Your Mother*. I reside in Rochester, NY.

Secrets
by Christy O'Callaghan

Elizabeth "Betty" Ann Sexton (1913-2007)

"**O**h no!"

I grab Dr. Forester's shirt sleeve and spread my legs as far as my dress will allow. I'd doubled up on belts and Kotex that morning, but blood and clots pool by my feet anyway. The pressure from below my naval releases, and my knees buckle. Spots dance in front of my eyes. My heart pounds in my ears.

"I'm so sorry, Dr. Forester. I'll clean that up," I mumble as I slide to the puddle on the hallway floor.

"Mrs. Sexton, are you alright? Get her to a room!" *I've never heard him shout before.*

Hands help me into a wheelchair. *Is my dress ruined? I don't have material to replace it.*

"Please locate Dr. Sexton," Dr. Forester commands one of the nurses.

"No! You can't." I reach for the nurse's arm. My hand is gray, and my fingernails, split from the constant typing, have turned blue. "Please don't take him off rounds. I don't want to get him in trouble." The nurse looks to Dr. Forester, and he nods.

I hold the nurse's cool hand to my sweaty face as they wheel me down the hall. She doesn't pull away. I make a mental note to find out her name to add to my Christmas card list. Every time I meet a new person at the Mayo Clinic, I add them to my list.

Hands help me to the bed. Someone piles blankets on me because I can't stop shivering. Dr. Forester examines between my legs. My cheeks warm from embarrassment and worry that I'll gush all over him. But my body feels too heavy to resist, and my heart's beating too fast. The nurse's hand is still in mine.

"Mrs. Sexton, how do you feel now?" Dr. Forester asks.

"Okay, sir." I try to sit up, but my bones feel too tired and dense to lift. The blankets are heavy and warm.

"Good...good." He frowns. Even his silver hair looks dull. "This must've been going on for a while."

"Uh, yes, sir. I've always had terrible menses, but they're getting worse."

"Are you finding it stressful working in the transcription pool?"

I shudder thinking of the windowless basement filled with rows of women striking their fingers against the keys. The constant staccato of clack and ding in my ears. No air moves in the smoke-filled room. My shoulders and neck ache every day from hunching over doctors' illegible chicken-scratch. No mistakes allowed. Doctors calling me *Betty* rather than Mrs. Sexton. They treat me like a nitwit when I ask for clarification. They put their hand on my behind or shoulders – *I'm a married woman with a college education!* Never Dr. Forester, though. That's why I ask to do his transcripts when I feel lousy.

"No, I'm fine," I say as cheerfully as I can muster, afraid he'll say I'm not fit to work.

He leans in and speaks softly. "This'll worsen. We need to call your husband in to make some decisions." I can smell the starch and cigar smoke on his shirt. It replaces the smell of liquid rust from my own body.

"Decisions?" Bile rises from my stomach. I force myself to sit up. "You can tell me about 'the decisions.'"

"We should have your husband here."

"Please, Dr. Forester."

He sighs. "You need to stop working, and we should proceed with a hysterectomy. Your fibroid tumors are causing the aggressive bleeding," he pulls down the skin under my eyes, "and you're anemic. I'm not even sure you could become pregnant at this point."

The nurse drapes a blanket over my back as his words sink in. Thunder cracks in my soul. *I'm already twenty-seven. No job? No baby? Am I even a woman?*

"What are my other options?" I ask, with every ounce of dignity I possess.

"That's it," he says softly, his gray eyes shifting to the floor. *Can this hurt him as much as it hurts me? Does he understand what that would do to my life?*

My wretched job is food and rent. Tom's the only resident receiving any financial assistance; all the others have their fathers to fall back on. My Tom put himself through school. His father bounces between being a roustabout and laboring in the coal mines. He doesn't have two pennies and wouldn't give them to us if he did. *How will we eat in these hard times? Will a man stay with a wife who can't give him a child? Will Tom?*

"But we're newlyweds. Since the Panic, there's no work, and I'm lucky to have this job. Neither's an option. Please, you can't tell Tom." The tears burn through. The nurse pulls me closer. She's soft and smells of lavender. *How do I convince him?*

Dr. Forester drones on about risks and dangers. "But this is *my* life," I whisper.

"Pardon me, Doctor," the nurse says. "May I speak with you?" He nods. She squeezes my shoulder as she leaves my side. The tears keep flowing. I think back to when I met Tom in college.

I had escorted my best girlfriend, Norma, to study with her math tutor in his dormitory. As Norma flirted away, a tall man walked in wearing pajamas. *Heavens to Betsy!* He smiled at me as he did a belly-whopper onto one of the beds. His blue-green eyes never broke away from me as he asked his roommate, "Who's your friend?"

"Oh, that's just Betty."

"Hi, 'Just Betty,' I'm Just Tom."

I rolled my eyes. "Norma, are you ready to go? It's almost curfew."

I disliked him immediately. After that, he kept showing up on outings. I asked around about who he dated, what his interests were, what he was like. People said he didn't date, he studied. He was a medical student and only joined in if I'd be there. Over time, his mind and smile won my heart. Tom's the most focused man I've ever met. I'd mistaken it for arrogance.

Dr. Forester returns. "It seems there's a recently-open position that may suit you. It could be a good fit with what I hear of your hostess talents, manners, smart way of dressing, and correspondence. I'll put in a word for you myself. Be at the Personnel Office first thing in the morning."

I don't ask what the job is. *Anything to get out of the transcription pool.*

"See you again in a week. The nurse will get you some iron pills. In the meantime, drink plenty of fluids, get some rest, eat meat, liver,

and fresh green vegetables. If this doesn't improve, we do it my way."
I say *yes* to everything, even though I know we can't afford meat and fresh vegetables.

The nurse helps me clean up.

"What's your name?" I ask.

"Abigail, ma'am."

"Thank you, Abigail. You saved me."

"Us ladies have to stick together."

As I walk to our apartment, I look at the dried, crusted blood on my shoes. They feel like part of the sidewalk. I stop every block to catch my breath and settle the dizziness. The doctor's recommendations tumble through my mind. I decide not to tell Tom. My heart hurts from the day and aches with knowing I will be keeping a secret from him.

The husband has the final say in all decisions – but only if he knows about them.

After struggling up the stairs, I scrub my shoes and soak my dress, stockings, and undergarments. *I must get them clean and hung to dry before Tom gets home.* I swallow a blackish-green iron pill so Tom won't see me take it with dinner. All I've had to eat today were the hospital cookies and juice hours earlier. The iron hits my stomach like a boulder and immediately forces itself back up into the sink. I slump to the floor and give myself the luxury of another good cry. *Crying doesn't cost anything.* As the bell strikes seven, I pull myself up and pat my hot puffy face with some cool tap water to add some color to my cheeks.

My brain spins as I force my way through my evening routine. I place a less-than-exciting dinner on the table, mostly foods from tins and some stewed pears Mother sent from her garden. Rounds of tears threaten, but I force them down and bring a smile to my face.

The door opens, and my heart flutters at seeing Tom, fearing he knows. He walks across the tiny kitchen in two long strides. Concern fills his eyes.

"My Betty," he says and wraps his arms around me as I rest my head against his chest. I can feel something in his jacket pocket as I melt against him. "I heard you had a rough day." He pulls me closer.

"What do you mean?" I tense, wanting to push him away, but don't.

"Dr. Forester told me you collapsed. It caused quite a commotion. How are you feeling?"

"Better, thank you. Such a fuss!" *What else did Dr. Forester tell you? Do you know? Are you waiting for me to tell you?* I pull away and steer him towards the table.

He doesn't press, instead announcing, "Wait, I have a gift."

"You shouldn't have bought anything," I smile.

I chuckle as he pulls out a bottle of Coke from his jacket. "Date night," he says as he hits the bottle on the edge of the table to pop off the cap. He pours half into each of our jelly jars.

The semester after we became serious, Norma and I managed to get a room over Tom's. When he wanted a break from his studies, he'd tap on the radiator pipe three times. We'd go for a walk and a Coke. Some of the girls thought this boring and unromantic. They wanted dancing, films, dinner, and gifts. I didn't miss any of that. We shared our stories, dreams, and goals. We fell in love over those Cokes. We made plans for a life together on those walks.

Tonight, I fall in love with him again over Mother's pears and jelly jars of Coke.

I can't lose this.

The next morning, I step into the Personnel Office, crammed with paper, overflowing ashtrays, and stained coffee mugs.

"Dr. Forester has strongly recommended you. He's well-respected, and I haven't received any complaints about you. Your husband has an excellent reputation. Did the doctor explain the position?"

It's the first time the man with slicked-back hair and thick glasses looks up from his desk. He slowly inspects me from shoes to hair. I blush, relieved I'd checked my strawberry-blond finger waves, pinched my cheeks, and touched up my lipstick before I came into the office. My body feels like I spent the night drinking highballs and being punched in my lower abdomen, but I sit up straight with my ankles crossed.

"No, sir. He said I'd be a good fit and, naturally, I was flattered. I'm proud to do my part for the Mayo Clinic." I smile, but not too broadly. *Friendly, not floozy,* as Mother would say.

"The role is to host our VIP patients. As you know, people come here from all over, and we need a Gal Friday to see to their needs, using the utmost discretion. Can you keep privacies, Mrs. Sexton?" He looks me in the eye.

I grip my hands tighter in my lap. *I'm keeping a big secret right now.* "Oh, yes, Mr. Meyers, I can be trusted to keep patients' privacies. Any doctor will tell you I treat patient information with the respect it deserves. My husband taught me the importance of confidentiality."

My stomach's doing little flips. *I can do this position. I must thank Abigail.*

"Would you be available to start today? This is a trial and, if all goes well, the position's yours." Mr. Meyers mentions a name, and I recall seeing it in the newspaper. He explains that the patient is this fellow's "secret girlfriend." *Oh, dear.* I write down his instructions. As he finishes, I recall seeing newspaper headlines with this man's name. He's reputed to be a gangster from Chicago, involved with robberies and possibly murders. I force my face to stay placid and not show my shock.

"There's one more thing." He opens a second file. "Normally, this would be a promotion and would come with a raise. However, your husband's a resident fellow."

"Yes, sir."

"I needn't remind you of the policy that a wife may not earn more than her husband." He looks at my eyes again, and I nod. "I want to make sure that's entirely clear. I don't want you coming back to my office crying or spreading gossip and discontent. You hear me? No making trouble. It won't serve you, the Mayo Clinic or, I dare say, your husband, to be overly dramatic about it."

I take a deep breath to calm myself and smile. *I need this job to save my life and my marriage.* "Sir, I appreciate the reminder. I won't disappoint you, the Mayo Clinic, or my husband. Now if you don't mind, there's a great deal to attend to." I rise, and he stands before me in wrinkled shirt and slacks. *I'd never allow my Tom to leave the house like that.* He puts out his hand, and I give it a firm shake – but not firmer than his. *Always be a lady.*

I spend the rest of the morning in town collecting the requested items, charging them to the hospital's tab, including makeup, curlers, robe, and flowers. I prepare the room thinking of the interior design books Tom's sister sends. My new supervisor inspects my work. He tells me I've done an excellent job for my first attempt and gives me a few pointers for next time. The VIPs are due any moment, and I'm to greet them at their car.

They arrive in a black limo. He steps out wearing a pinstriped suit, taller and broader than he looks in photographs. *I'm five-and-a-half-feet, and I just reach his pocket square!* A tiny blond creature emerges, looking like a child playing dress-up. Her bones and blue veins show through her pale skin. I wonder if it's lack of food or her illness. I don't ask; it's none of my business.

Kitty, as I'll call her, puts her frail arm around mine, her delicate fingers grip above my elbow. She chatters the entire walk to her room. I'm not sure what to say. I'm not used to being around criminals and mistresses. *What do I have in common with this woman?* I smile and nod, giggle when necessary. Her beau praises my boss for the accommodations, but Kitty whispers, "You did this. I sense a woman's touch."

"If you gentlemen don't mind, I'd like to help the lady settle in." Once they leave, Kitty collapses on the bed. Smile and chatter gone, she looks even younger and smaller. I unpack her bags and put out some magazines.

"Is there anything else I can get for you?"

"Can you keep him busy? He means well but gets upset when I'm not okay. I don't have the energy to smile for him one more minute." I can feel her exhaustion in my body, but hesitate. *What if the stories about him are true?* I see the circles under her eyes and remember why I must do this. *C'mon, Betty. That man stands between you and this job. Kitty's just another woman trying to survive. You can do this. You can save your life. And maybe hers.*

"Of course," I smile and squeeze her hand. *Us ladies have to stick together.*

I let the staff know they can proceed with Kitty, and I show her beau to the cafeteria. I give him a tour as we walk, my quick steps keeping up with his long strides. He barely looks at me, instead chewing on an unlit cigar and staring at his highly-shined wingtips. *He's worried. This is what Tom would look like if it were me. It is me – Tom just doesn't know.* I notice all the stares at the looming figure walking next to me and want to shout, *He's not as scary as he looks.* I leave him with a cup of coffee dwarfed by his giant paw. To keep him company, I send over a few cafeteria girls I pal around with.

When I return to the room, I sit with Kitty and hold her hand as the doctors and nurses continue to work. When they finish, I bring her beau back to say good night. I wait outside in the hallway, planning for the next day.

"Thanks, sweetheart. Take good care of my girl." He winks as he leaves the room.

She's asleep with a magazine laid open across her chest. I place it on her bedside table and pull up her covers. My boss is standing at the nurses' station as I leave.

"Good work today, Mrs. Sexton. Dr. Forester said you'd be a good fit, and I agree. Oh, our friend said his girl is quite taken with you. He left this." My supervisor pulls a large bottle from behind the desk.

"Am I allowed to take that? Will I get fired?" The bottle probably cost more than a couple months' rent.

"Tokens, yes. Cash, no. You earned it. But don't expect it every time."

Relief fills my tired body as I try to hide the bottle in my purse. Tonight, we'll celebrate with potted meat, Mother's preserved peaches, and jelly jars of champagne. We'll talk and toast to our unknown future: Tom will go off to war, we'll relocate several times, change careers, and buy a home. And finally, after eight more years, we'll have the baby girl I always wanted.

Christy O'Callaghan: My grandmother and I were so different from each other, yet very much alike. She admired my rebellious spirit, although she never recognized it in herself. I share the same health issues as Betty, so I realize how hard it was for her to create the life she wanted. Writing *Secrets* gave me a chance to reminisce with my mom and quilt together stories we'd heard; it was like we were visiting with my grandmother. I'm a member of the Hudson Valley Writers Guild, and my writing has appeared in *Perspectives Magazine* and *Saved Objects*. I live in Amsterdam, NY, and you can find me on Instagram @christyflutterby.

Sergeant Rogers Reports for Duty
by Donna Jackel

Marie Rogers Jackel (1918-2002)

2 April 1940

I am too excited to sleep tonight. No more sitting on the sidelines while the Nazis burn down Jewish businesses and force my people to sew yellow Stars of David on their clothes! Tomorrow, I enlist in the Women's Auxiliary Air Force.

3 April 1940

My life has changed completely in one day! I will be leaving my position as a legal secretary to serve my country. The hard part will be breaking the news to Mum and Daddy.

Later that day...

Tonight, at dinner, I burst out, "I've enlisted in the Women's Auxiliary!"

For once, Toby and Rita had nothing to say. My younger sisters just stared at me.

Mummy's face turned pale, then bright red.

"You will have to tell them you cannot go!"

Silence. Then Daddy offered quietly, in his thick accent, "Marie is 21. If she has enlisted, it cannot be undone."

I tried to make Mum understand. "Look what the Germans are doing to the Jews! This is our war! I want to be a part of it."

She only grew angrier. "I never expected to see a daughter in uniform! You're deserting the family!"

I ran up to my bedroom to cry. Later, I tiptoed into Daddy's studio where his head was bent over his sewing machine. He looked up to see me hovering in the doorway and smiled. "Come here, Marie. Let me take your measurements – I want you should have the finest uniform in the Auxiliary."

I threw my arms around him. He whispered, "Please be careful. I don't know what I would do if anything happened to you."

5 June 1940

Tomorrow, I report to Cranwell Air Force Base in Lincolnshire, about 165 kilometers from home. It is one of several Royal Air Force training schools charged with rapidly preparing our air defense. The WAAFs will be trained to pack parachutes, repair planes, and operate radar, among other duties. Because of my business skills, I will be personal secretary to Cranwell's commanding officer, Air Commodore D. Harries.

25 June 1940

Commodore Harries is a physically imposing man, but a quiet soul, never uttering three words if two will do. He is kind to me and says he is impressed with my work.

10 July 1940

I am beginning to make friends with the women and men here. It is bittersweet knowing that some of the young pilots will not survive.

7 September 1940

Last night, London was under siege for hours. When it was over, hundreds of civilians were dead or seriously injured. What if Great Britain is defeated? I will try to remember Churchill's words: "Victory at all costs, victory in spite of all terror, victory, however long and hard the road may be; for without victory, there is no survival."

15 November 1940

I don't think I can bear another day like this. Last night, the Germans bombed Coventry for ten hours. Since the city is less than 30 kilometers from Birmingham, I was worried about my family. I rang home repeatedly but couldn't get through. Imagining the worst – our house bombed, my family lying injured or dead in the rubble –

I went to Commodore H. and requested an emergency pass. When I got off the train at Coventry, volunteers were lifting limp bodies from the wreckage.

A kind deliveryman gave me a lift to Birmingham. When I finally reached Varner Road, it looked unscathed. I ran inside our house to find my family calmly unpacking food from cartons, having just returned from an air raid shelter. In my relief, I hugged Mum fiercely.

"What's all this?" she wanted to know.

I was so relieved to find them safe that I began to laugh and cry at the same time.

We had a quick tea. I was so happy to be home with my loved ones that it didn't rile me when Rita piped up, "How come you're in the Air Force, but we're the ones who keep getting bombed?"

22 November 1940

The bombs rained down on Birmingham for 11 hours. The city is vulnerable to attack because it has several munitions factories. Each time Birmingham is attacked, I'm terrified until Daddy calls.

24 March 1941

Wonderful news – I've been promoted to sergeant! In addition to my office work, I am in charge of a platoon of WAAFs.

3 June 1941

Commodore H. called me into his office to tell me that a woman in my squad is quite pregnant. As if that weren't shock enough, he accused me of keeping her pregnancy a secret! I pointed out that Sarah is quite heavy, which made it impossible to detect her pregnancy. At that, Commodore H. turned bright red and gazed at his shoes. Sarah will be discharged and, hopefully, this is the last I will hear of the matter.

7 December 1941

Gail, Izzy, and I were at the Golden Crown celebrating my 22nd birthday when a roar rippled through the crowd. America has joined the war! The Japanese attacked a U.S. military base in Hawaii. The States can sit on the fence no more.

1 January 1942

It's been raining all day. I lie on my bed trying to read, but I can't concentrate. It's nearly two years since I arrived in Lincolnshire, and I am increasingly restless. I have applied for several transfers, to no avail. I miss my parents and sisters. Although I have friends here, I often feel lonely.

22 June 1942

Gail, Izzy, and I were on our way to the Canteen when dozens of green flares began falling from the sky. As we ran to the nearest bomb shelter, Gail became hysterical. I grabbed her hand, and we dove in. After an hour or so, the all-clear sounded. We returned to duty, a little shaken but none the worse. War is terrifying and unpredictable, yet makes me appreciate every moment.

2 September 1942

I have applied for a six-month training course at Cambridge University. Maybe this is the opportunity I've been hoping for.

2 October 1942

I leave for Cambridge next week! I will miss all my friends here, but I'm ready for a new adventure.

4 November 1942

We are learning to administer psychological tests to Air Force recruits. These personality tests will be used to determine which men possess the necessary qualities to be fighter pilots – aggressive and outgoing – and which are better suited to be bomber pilots – calm and steady.

3 December 1942

I have arrived in London for my first assignment. I shed tears of anger at first sight of the shattered city. But I am heartened by the resilience of the British; rebuilding is already underway.

Last night, Gail and I went to a dance at the American Officers Club where I met a young fighter pilot, Sgt. David Toporofsky, a Polish-American Jew. He's a fine dancer and, unlike other American servicemen I've met, refreshingly down-to-earth. He confided that he's homesick. I ventured, "It must be very hard to be so far from home" and tenderly squeezed his hand.

3 June 1943

David and I held hands in the cinema while watching *For Whom the Bell Tolls*. I leaned my head on his shoulder. Common sense tells me to take it slow, but my heart...

28 June 1943

David is on a mission tonight. I cannot sleep.

30 June 1943

David is back! This afternoon, we had a picnic in the countryside. He looked terrible – deep circles under his eyes. I brought a hamper of whatever I could lay my hands on – black bread, cheese, and dried fruit. David was so pleased that I was able to unearth a bottle of red wine. He was very quiet, which I attribute to battle fatigue. Since he isn't permitted to discuss his mission, he talked about his parents and sister and their life in New York City. The more time we spend together, the stronger my feelings become. I wish I had a clearer sense of his feelings for me.

19 September 1943

Tomorrow, I leave for Edinburgh where I will be stationed for months.

15 October 1943

A wonderful three-day visit with Daddy! We walked all over Edinburgh and enjoyed a kosher meal. Daddy didn't say a word when I spilled chicken soup down the front of the uniform he'd made – *lokshen* hanging on my shiny brass buttons! When I introduced him to my friends, they asked if he is my boyfriend because he looks so young!

We had serious moments, too. Daddy told me he is glad Grandpa is dead so the Nazis can't get him. But he worries about the rest of his family in Poland; he fears he will never see them again.

7 June 1944

Glorious news! The Allies landed in Normandy yesterday to begin the liberation. I pray for these brave men.

20 September 1944

Tomorrow, David returns home on leave. I want to tell him I love him, but I'm determined not to be the first to say it. Who knows when we will see one another again?

10 November 1944

I received a four-page letter from David. He writes that he will not return to combat, no matter the consequences:

Marie, I'm ashamed to admit that I've become afraid of airplanes – totally, completely, crazily afraid. No doubt experienced fliers are needed, but a man who is afraid is no use to his crew. Better, I think, that one man be punished than the lives of nine other men endangered.

In a postscript, he writes that he is being reclassified to air-gunning instructor, serving stateside. I know I should be happy – this means he will be safe for the remainder of the war, which we are clearly winning. But I miss him! While the tone of his letter is warm, it's signed, *As ever, David.* No love.

11 March 1945

I have been shut up in my bedroom. I don't want anyone to see my swollen eyes. David sent me a *Dear Jane* letter. He has fallen in love with someone else. I feel angry, betrayed! We never made firm promises, but I thought we had an understanding. My only comfort is that I never told my family about him, so there is no need to tell them we are no more.

21 April 1945

Man's inhumanity to man! Now I understand the meaning of that Robert Burns poem. At the cinema, they ran a newsreel of British troops liberating Bergen-Belsen concentration camp. Living ghosts stood behind barbed-wire fencing. Behind them lay mounds of unburied corpses, just skin stretched over bones. I ran to the bathroom and vomited until my stomach was empty. How could the Nazis murder women and children? How do we not lose all hope given the depths of human evil?

22 April 1945

Berlin is under siege by the Russians. It is only a matter of time until Germany officially surrenders!

7 May 1945

VE Day is tomorrow, but people are already singing and drinking in the streets! At home, we enjoy a quiet celebration: Roast turkey, Toby's mince pie, and a toast to our prime minister.

9 May 1945

All five of us gathered around the wireless to hear Churchill officially announce the end of the European war. He told the enormous crowd gathered at Whitehall, "This is your victory!" They roared back, "No, it's yours!" We all cried, but this time in happiness.

6 June 1945

My wool uniform is packed away in mothballs. I served my country for 5-1/4 years. There were times I fought boredom and depression. I second-guessed myself – had I been right to enlist, or should I have remained home with my family? But, all in all, I am gratified by my decision. I left my sheltered, insular life in Birmingham, learned how to be self-sufficient, and to get along with all kinds of people.

5 July 1945

Thanks to my wartime training, I have landed an interesting, well-paying position with the Social Survey, which collects data to monitor national trends. I will travel around the country interviewing citizens on different subjects and then report my results.

I told Mum my good news this afternoon, but she only grumbled, "Why do you have to leave home again?"

30 July 1945

I'm off to Penarth, South Wales for my first assignment. I will be surveying the coal miners on their attitudes about their jobs. The British government wants to know whether there will be enough miners in the future to support the coal industry.

23 August 1945

There is no way to prepare for the total darkness and dankness that greets you as you enter a mine shaft. Extracting coal from deep below the ground is dirty, dangerous, backbreaking labor. The miners arrive home each night coughing and covered in coal dust. It's no surprise many don't want their sons to follow them into this line of work – even if it means they will have to leave home to earn a living.

22 March 1946

Mum phoned me yesterday. Daddy had a cold when he entered the hospital for a routine checkup on his ulcer. Now, that cold has turned into pleurisy.

30 March 1946

I called home to check on Daddy, and Rita's husband, Mick, answered. He would only say, "You'd better come home, Marie." Now I'm on a 13-hour train ride to Birmingham, trying to calm my nerves by knitting a sweater for Daddy.

Later that day...

Mick met me at the train station. "You'd better sit down," he said.

My heart began pounding.

"I'm sorry, Marie. Your father is dead. He was buried yesterday. I thought it best to tell you in person."

"No," I said softly. "No."

2 April 1946

I spoke with Daddy's physician. I needed to know how a relatively-healthy 56-year-old man could deteriorate so quickly. Apparently, a new drug to treat infections, penicillin, was prescribed for him. He had an allergic reaction to it, followed by a fatal heart attack. I can't believe I'll never see him again.

3 April 1946

Uncle Percy tells me there were so many people at Daddy's funeral that they flowed out the front door onto the street. This is comforting, but I don't know whether I can forgive my family for not calling me to his side sooner.

10 April 1946

I am asking for a transfer to Birmingham. My family needs me. And I need them.

19 November 1946

I awoke this morning feeling such sadness, like a heavy load pressing on my chest. I took the train to Brighton Beach to clear my head.

Everything was gray – the sky, the ocean, the pebbles beneath my feet. I'd never felt so alone. I walked along the beach, sobbing loudly, a cold wind at my back. There was no one to hear me but the seagulls. I thought of Daddy, of David. I stepped closer to the water's edge. Since I can't swim, I knew the strong waves could easily knock me down and drag me under. No more pain. But then I thought of Mum, Toby, and Rita, still in mourning, waiting for me to come home. I returned to the warmth of the train station.

2 February 1947

Mum is slowly surfacing from her deep grief. She has agreed to accompany me to New York City to meet members of Daddy's family who immigrated there before the war. The trip will be good for both of us. We have booked passage on the RMS Queen Mary.

4 April 1947

I have found a soul mate in my first cousin, Goldie Tannenbaum, a strong, kind, intelligent woman. We are staying with her and her husband, Willie, in the Bronx. They have taken us to meet family and see the sights – the Statue of Liberty, the Empire State Building, and several Broadway shows.

10 June 1947

Mum and I were due to sail home next week, but Goldie has convinced me to extend my visit. I've taken a secretarial job at the British Embassy. It is dull, and the pay is abysmal, but jobs are scarce these days.

13 May 1948

As much as I love Goldie, I have decided to return to England. I miss my family, my country. I booked passage for August 14.

4 June 1948

What a lovely surprise! I ran into Gwen, one of my dearest friends in the WAAF. We are going to a dance at the Diplomat Hotel tomorrow evening.

7 June 1948

Again, my life has changed completely in one day!

I was ready to leave the dance –it was a dull crowd – when I heard a man's voice directly behind me.

"Would you like to dance?"

I whirled around to find a slender young man with soft brown eyes and curly auburn hair smiling at me. As we danced, we found we have much in common: We're both Jewish. We've both recently lost our fathers. We both served in World War II. He is in law school, and I've worked as a legal secretary.

We went out for coffee. We chatted easily. Max insisted on taking me all the way home to the Bronx on the subway. I invited him up for a coffee.

We sat in Goldie's kitchen at the Formica table. I took the lid off the milk bottle, and it fell in. I had a dickens of a time fishing it out, but I persisted.

"There!" I announced, smiling and holding up the lid triumphantly.

Max smiled at me affectionately, as if we've known each other for years instead of a few hours. He shook his head and laughed.

"What's so funny?"

"What have I gotten myself into? You're one determined woman!"

And just like that, I knew Max Jackel was the man I would marry.

Donna Jackel: World War II briefly opened up opportunities for women to prove they were as capable as men. My mother was modest and didn't often mention her years of service in the Women's Auxiliary Air Force. The skills she attained enabled her to secure a well-paying, interesting, post-war position. Marie (pronounced *Mar-ee*) died at the age of 82 – I wish she were here to read her story. I'm a Rochester, NY-based freelance journalist, focusing on animal welfare, mental health, and social justice. My work has been published in regional and national publications, including *The Chicago Tribune, Lilith Magazine, BBC Travel,* and *The Bark.*

Worth So Much More
by Barbara J. Spaeth

Frances Elizabeth Knoll (1923-2017)

I pause, taking a deep breath to calm my nerves. I've arrived at work early to avoid being seen entering the Union president's office. I place my letter on his desk, relieved no one else is there yet. I slide into my chair to begin typing. I'm amazed I can decipher the shorthand I took during that dreadful session yesterday. I could type a lot faster if I could stop shaking. Perhaps I should just quit right now.

I only hope I won't have to be alone with my boss today. Giving one week's notice is the right thing to do. It's the only thing I can do.

I'm typing as fast as I can when I feel someone standing next to me. *Oh, no! He's here again!* But it's Mr. Burns, the Union president, with a stern look on his face. This is not typical; he's always been so nice to me.

"Frances, please come into my office right now."

As I enter his office, he motions for me to sit down. He seats himself, narrows his eyes, and asks, "Why are you leaving?"

I'm at a loss. I hadn't thought this through. It had never occurred to me that anyone would care why I was leaving. I'm just a secretary.

I hesitate. "I can't tell you." *Where is a good lie when you need one?* The guilt and embarrassment are too much to admit to anyone, especially someone I respect and admire as much as Mr. Burns.

"You need to tell me what happened. You're not leaving! The entire office relies on you."

I mumble something to get out of his office and return to the safety of my desk.

I got so little sleep last night that I can't concentrate on transcribing yesterday's dictation. My mind keeps going back over the past few weeks: *How did this all begin? How could I have stopped the unwanted passes from my boss?* At first, I was just a little put off by his behavior. He started out by complimenting my appearance. One day, he commented, "Frances, you have great legs. You should wear that dress more often."

If a man had said that to me at a dance, I might have been flattered, but his tone made me uncomfortable. I could feel my face turn red, yet I remained polite as I replied, "Thank you." But I felt like slapping him. *What kind of girl does he think I am? He's not my type at all. I'd never date anyone who is short, chubby, and married!*

A few days later, he probed, "What are you doing after work?"

My stomach churning, I replied, "I'm expected at my sister Alice's tonight to look after my nieces." It wasn't totally a lie.

His response of "Perhaps tomorrow?" unnerved me. But I'd managed to keep him at bay until yesterday when I was summoned to his small office to take a letter. He usually dictates seated, and I feel a little safer with that massive desk between us. This time, as he started the dictation, he got up, walked around the desk, closed the door, touched my back as he brushed by me, and sat on top of the desk, looming over me. As he continued the dictation, he rubbed my arm. I felt trapped, thinking of the closed door behind me. I bolted before he finished the letter. "The usual closing?" I asked over my shoulder as I grabbed the door knob and flew out. Later, he made a point to walk by my desk, putting a hand on my shoulder with a slight squeeze, like we'd just shared something special. My stomach flipped over.

I've had enough of this jerk!

The worst part is that I really love this job. I'm the only woman working at the Independent Leather Workers' Union in Gloversville, New York. The Union is essential to the people in a town dependent on the glove and leather industries. Before the Union, the working conditions were horrendous, especially in the tanneries. I know I'm only a secretary, but, in my mind, my job helps all the workers and their families.

This is a far cry from the future my father and I had planned when I was ten years old. My father was an accomplished pianist and, during one of our weekly piano lessons, when I had him all to myself, we'd planned a nursing career for me. The local hospital offered a top-notch training program, and I couldn't wait to grow up. My father was a gentle and resourceful man, supporting a family of six children during the Depression. Somehow, he managed to support my dream at the same time. That dream died along with my Dad when I was fourteen. My life was never the same.

This issue at work is all my mother's fault! If only she'd let me finish high school. She's the one who insisted I quit school two years ago. In fact, she quit for me! I arrived home from high school one afternoon, and she told me, in a matter-of-fact way, "Frances, I was able to get you a job at the grocery store. You are finished with high school."

"What about my plans for nursing school?"

Mom screamed. (She rarely used any other tone of voice when she and I were together.) "You're a woman. Education is wasted on women. Once you're married, you won't be working anyway. Right now, we need money to support this family!"

We screamed at each other until I ran out of the house, slamming the door. There was nothing to be done. She made it clear that I was to help support the family or go out on my own. I spent the weekend at Alice's house to let things cool down.

I didn't understand why she couldn't manage to support us. Only my younger brother and I were left at home. My two older brothers were on their own, and my sisters were married. Mom took in piecework, sewing gloves. We also had a couple of boarders to help with rent.

Damn, she must hate me to have stripped me of my dream to be a nurse!

Wasting no time, I came up with an alternative plan for my future. Gloversville High School offered secretarial courses at night. I kept that stupid job at the grocers until I got my certificate in shorthand, typing, and bookkeeping. With that in hand, and help from my older brother, Ernie, I was able to get this respectable job with the Union.

But then this unwanted attention began. I tried to figure out how I could save my job and my self-respect. I had lunch with my best friend and confided in her. Eileen was sympathetic but could only encourage me to quit. "It's the only thing you can do. If you don't go along, he'll fire you. So, you're out of a job anyway. Just make sure you don't tell anyone."

"It's just not fair. I deserve to keep my job."

Eileen was getting exasperated with me, making clear my other choice: "Well, you could have an affair with him!"

I'd considered asking Ernie for advice. He's the sports editor for the *Leader Republican* newspaper and knows everyone. He tries his best to look out for me – he even found me a boyfriend! (However, I saw no future with a boy who would not dance.) I went to Ernie's office during lunch the other day to ask his advice. The room was filled with newspaper activity: Typing, cigarette smoke, lots of chatter, and men. All men. I decided this wasn't the time or place for this discussion. I could picture my brother laughing and telling me I was imagining things. He's not known for keeping a confidence. The boys in the newsroom would have had a big laugh at my expense.

I wondered if either of my older sisters might offer some advice on how to deal with the situation. I spend lots of time with them and their families. But, after much thought, I decided that since they had never held jobs, they would have no idea what it's like to be nineteen, single, and working for a disgusting rat who won't leave you alone.

I'm on my own. As usual. *Oh, Dad, where are you when I need you?*

Ultimately, I made my own decision: I will resign. My mother will be furious, but I will not compromise my integrity for this job. She would never understand this situation. In fact, she'd tell me it's all my fault. She always criticizes what I wear and the way I do my hair. I love to dress like the movie stars; they're so glamourous! But she tells me they are too risqué. This from a woman who was a Gibson Girl model in New York City.

But now, I must stop rehashing the past and get some work done. If I keep pacing around the room, I'll get fired for not working. Since it seems this day will never end, I don't know how I'll make it to the end of the week. I've managed to turn one problem into two. Not only am I fearful that my jerk of a boss will get me alone again, now Mr. Burns is angry with me for resigning. I just need to focus on my work, and how good it will feel to be away from that shmuck, once and for all.

How many more sleepless nights until Friday?

* * *

Just one more cup of coffee, and I can get through another day. But I barely get in the door when Mr. Burns calls me into his office again. As soon as the door closes, he barks, "Frances, you need to tell me why you're quitting. You are not leaving my office until you give me a good explanation. This office runs smoothly because of you. I don't want to lose you."

With tears in my eyes, I stammer, "I can't tell you. I'm too embarrassed to explain. Just let me quit and get on with my life."

He gives me a reassuring look. In a tone that reminds me of my father, he says, "You can tell me. It will be alright. There must be something I can do to keep you from leaving."

I try to think of something to tell him. Anything that will get me out of this predicament without telling the truth. But I can no longer avoid it. I'm doing everything I can not to cry when I blurt out, "My boss is making passes at me, and I can't take it anymore!"

The look on his face makes it clear this is not a surprise. He nods. "Go back to work. I will handle this."

Mr. Burns seems to understand. I'm feeling a little better. Although still worried, at least I know my work has value. Perhaps I will still have a career here.

* * *

Finally, a good night's sleep. I was too exhausted to stay awake. But now, my doubts return: *What if my boss just gets reprimanded? Will he try to retaliate? What if he denies everything?* I could always just walk out, but everyone would know.

Things seem odd this morning as I rush into the office. The room is buzzing with excitement, people are standing around, and the creep is nowhere to be seen. One of the workers asks, "Fran, did you hear the news? The boss just got fired! He stormed out just before you got here. No one knows why."

Relief floods my body. Not only do I feel safe at work again, but I realize my work is valued. The Union president was willing to sack my boss – a man – before letting me go! I have kept my job and my self-respect.

I'm not sure if this job is my future. I'm not sure what lies ahead for me. But I will never let anyone treat me like that again. I'm worth so much more.

Barbara J. Spaeth: Although my mother always loved to tell her stories, in later life, she'd only shrug when asked to repeat one. She passed away at the age of 93, just a few months prior to my writing this story about her courage and dignity. Women's rights in the workplace were not a consideration in the early 1940s; the term *sexual harassment* wasn't part of our vocabulary. By putting myself in her place, I was able to connect with her again, an emotionally-healing experience. I'm a retired elementary school teacher, currently serving on the board of the Sacandaga Valley Arts Network, where I chair the Music Committee. My husband and I live in Northville, NY.

Always with Me
by Zoe Ann Christensen Gonza

Rosalie Girard Christensen (1931-2011)

My dad comes home very tired from the Gouverneur Talc Mine every evening – especially lately. My brother and I do many of the chores so he can nap after work.

Being a twelve-year-old in 1943, I'm very busy with school, friends, and my daily household duties. My family is not wealthy, but we have a nice house and a lot of love.

My mom is busy with church and housework, along with her most important job (as she says) of raising my older brother, Carl, and me to be "good and respectful children." Going to school is one of my favorite things. I do very well, which makes my parents proud. My greatest wish is to someday go to college and become a teacher.

I talk to my friends about classwork and boys during our long walks to and from school. Lately, though, I talk more about my dad. "I'm so scared because he looks so thin. My mom tells me that sometimes men lose weight at his age because they're working so hard. But I'm pretty sure she's just saying this because she thinks I'm too young to handle anything bad." My friends listen but don't know what to say.

Today, I come home to find my dad in bed. My mom is crying in the kitchen but quickly wipes away her tears when she hears me walk in. "Why is Dad home already?" I ask.

"Rosalie, I can see the worry on your face, but you mustn't let it consume you. Your dad started coughing so hard at work that he went to see the mining company doctor. They did a chest x-ray at the hospital and then told him to take the rest of the day off."

My eyes fill with tears and, even though my mom is telling me not to worry, I have a feeling that something terrible is going to happen. I'm trying so hard to appear positive. It's taking all I have to not add to my mother's stress by showing how depressed I am.

I'm glad it's the weekend so my dad can relax, but as strong-willed as he is, he gets up early to mow the lawn and do odd jobs around the house. This weekend is different, though. My brother and my dad are spending a lot of time together. I overhear my father telling Carl how the coal furnace works. He then explains how the refrigerator and gas stove work. I ask Carl, "Why do you think Dad is teaching you how to operate and fix every single thing in and outside of our home?" Carl proudly responds, "Dad feels I'm old enough to be doing some of the man's work around the house."

His reply makes me mad because I could do the things Carl is being taught. I'd much prefer stoking the coal and mowing the lawn than helping my mom with dusting and cleaning. I'm also worried about Dad's health. I know deep inside that's the real reason he is sharing the details of his duties. I also wonder if Carl is trying to protect me, or does he not see what I see?

On Sunday morning, we go to St. James Church. Speaking with Father Shue after Mass, Mom says, "Father, would you like to join us for breakfast? It won't be much, but we'd love to have you." Father accepts, saying, "I'd be honored. The company of your family is a most precious gift." When he arrives, we divide up the small piece of ham our family received from Aunt Betty and cook up eggs from our own chickens. Dad tells Father Shue about our Sunday traditions. "We do all our chores on Saturday so Sunday is a day to spend with family. One of our Sunday routines is that I let Carl practice driving down the road. I never leave him alone in the car, but it'll make him a better driver someday. Rosalie's treat is that I make her a special cup of coffee. It's mostly milk, of course."

As he tells Father Shue about my Sunday treat, I think back to all the years of sitting on my dad's lap to drink it. That is one of my favorite traditions. Little do I know that this will be one of the last Sundays when I get to drink my special coffee.

Dad continues to go to work but comes home more tired by the week. He now coughs all day. I overhear him tell Mom that he was told by the work doctor that his chest x-ray is nothing to worry about. When Carl gets home from school, seeing how tired Dad is, he begins doing all the jobs that Dad used to do around the house.

I try to let my schoolwork distract me from the worry I constantly have about my dad's illness. The last thing I want is for my grades to drop, but I find that most days I'm quiet and distracted. "He's not getting better," I tell my friends. "He's lost so much weight and is so pale. Seeing him so out-of-breath scares me." My best friend, Rena, gives me a hug and, trying not to cry herself, says, "Rosalie, I love you and will help any way I can." But there is nothing she or anyone can do.

It's a Sunday after church when Mom and Dad sit Carl and me down to have a family meeting. Mom has tears in her eyes as Dad tells us, "I'm afraid my breathing problem is so bad that I won't be able to work full time anymore. It makes me feel terrible, but your mom will be looking for a job now."

My throat tightens, tears fill my eyes. This announcement means huge changes for our family. We will no longer have our mom waiting for us when we arrive home from school. Who will make supper on days she has to work late? Most importantly, if Dad is home sick, will I be capable of taking care of him? I keep telling myself that I can't add more worry to my parents' lives by being overly concerned, but I am overcome with fear and grief. I know I have to be strong and quickly learn to do more to help out.

Mom writes down some of our favorite recipes – bean soup, homemade bread, macaroni and cheese, creamed beef on toast. I begin to cook most of our family's meals with Mom's guidance. A couple of times, I forget to plan for our supper, so last-minute ketchup sandwiches are served. Nobody complains – there's too much else to worry about.

Mom now has a job working downtown for a nice man at his shoe store. Since she doesn't drive, she walks to the store each day and works as many hours as her boss will allow. Dad has decided he can no longer work at the talc mine; he is so tired and can't catch his breath. He spends more and more time sleeping on the couch in the living room. There are too many stairs to climb to the bedroom. "This couch is plenty comfortable. I want to be with my family as much as possible. This is also easier when friends and neighbors stop by to say hello."

Seeing how hard our mom is working at the shoe store, Carl decides to get a job. He is hired by the local lumber mill and works for three hours after school each day and on weekends. My parents and I feel sorry he has to give up playing school sports to do this for our family.

This leaves me with more responsibility around the house and, more importantly, gives me a lot of private time with my dad. We have many hours of conversation during which he shares the visions he has for my brother's and my future. He says I am an exceptionally smart girl and believes I can do anything I have my heart set on.

Finally, Dad tells me he is dying – something I have suspected for a long time but tried not to think about. Every day, we talk openly about it. Dad promises, "Rosalie, there will be signs that I'll always be with you." When I ask, "What kind of signs?" he hugs me and says, "Trust me. You'll see."

I am nervous but so grateful for these talks. He is preparing me for the inevitable. We say our daily prayers together before Mom and Carl get home for supper, which makes me less depressed.

Over the weeks, our talks get shorter. Dad sleeps most of the time. He holds my hand and opens his eyes, but he has no strength to talk. As he looks at me with so much love in his eyes, I know he is saying goodbye. My aunt and neighbors stay with him while Carl and I are at school and Mom's at work. I hate to leave him and worry about him the whole time I'm gone. My heart is breaking. I cry myself to sleep every night.

He doesn't open his eyes anymore. Mom says he is in a coma, but we all continue to whisper words of love in his ear. She lets Carl and me stay home from school so we can sit with Dad for as long as we want.

The most dreaded day arrives. Dad passes away at the age of thirty-nine. Mom, Carl, and I are with him as he takes his last breath. We hug each other and cry for hours. After that day, I do not see Mom shed a tear. It is so hard, but I am trying to be as strong and brave as she is.

The wake is held in the same room where Dad died. Neighbors, friends, and relatives come to pay their respects. I stand at the door with Mom to greet every single one of them. I don't know what to say, so I repeat what my mother says: "Thank you for coming."

As the weeks pass, my shattered heart begins to heal. I throw myself into my schoolwork and continue to get good grades in spite of all that's happened in my life. My work around the house does not lessen. Carl and Mom continue to work so we can pay our bills. My job now is to support and care for them.

In church one Sunday, singing at the beginning of the service, I hear my Dad's strong, beautiful voice: *Amazing grace, How sweet the sound.* I look around to discover that there are no men anywhere near us. The music finishes, and I remember it was one of Dad's favorite hymns. I know he is giving me a sign that he is close to me, just like he said he would. I am so thrilled, but I don't tell my mom because I don't want her or my brother to think I'm crazy.

After we arrive home, my mom calls me to the table. At my seat is a hot cup of coffee with lots of milk. I start to cry and ask, "Why did you make me the treat Dad always gave me? You've never done that before." She replies, "Your dad spoke to me in church and told me it might cheer you up."

I feel signs of his presence nearly every day now. He is always with me, just as he promised. I'll never be able to afford college as I'd dreamed, but the memory of my dad's words of confidence in me are always in my thoughts.

Zoe Ann Christensen Gonza: This story was the most influential event of my mother's childhood, shaping her character forever. In retelling the story as she would have told it, I felt very close to that young-child version of her. It helped me get a clearer understanding of the impact that the loss she suffered at such a tender age had on my own childhood and on my personality. After a 40-year career as a nurse, I retired to care for my father following the death of my mom. My teachers always told me that I should become a writer. And now I am! I live in Syracuse, NY with my husband.

Southern Saratoga Soul
by Carol R. Daggs

Ruth R. Daggs (1931-present)

I never knew my father. He wasn't part of our lives and passed away before I began school. My mother's pet name is Missy. It's common for senior folk in familiar circles to address a younger girl by that name.

Mother supports our family through farm work: Harvesting sweet potatoes, white potatoes, and peanuts. She fashioned me a mode of transport that also serves as a way to collect her earthen treasures. I sit in a strong cardboard box while she pulls me alongside her. Up and down the rows, hauling a paper wagon without wheels, Mother passes potatoes in my direction. She studies her harvest and exclaims, "Looka here, Ruth. With the bacon we gots, these fine taters gonna make some good eatin' tonight!"

Our two-bedroom home with kitchen, fireplace, and hearth for cooking stands on a large lot in Beaufort, South Carolina. Relatives live nearby and have an outhouse. The grapefruit tree growing in the yard bears juicy, bright-yellow fruit we enjoy late summer into fall.

It's becoming increasingly difficult for Mother to manage everything and provide for the three of us. Little education, no spousal support, and inconsistent work all make poverty our reality. Hand-me-downs and goodwill from church folk kind enough to offer their gently-used items are gratefully received. Fortunately, Mother's two sisters live nearby and are able to help care for us.

Christmas remains a joyful, although meager, time for our family. Thankfully, we have plenty of love. My younger sisters and I each get stockings full of pecans, oranges, and peppermint candies.

Especially thrilling this year, there's a brown-skinned, bald-headed baby doll peering out over the top of my stocking. Quickly grabbing the doll, letting the other goodies fall to the floor, I exclaim in delight, "Mama, Mama! Look at my pretty little baby doll!"

"Yes. And y'all my pretty l'il babies."

As the seasons allow, Mother spends time between the fields and waterfront to supply our meals. "Ruth, we goin' to the shrimp dock today," she calls out. "Get yoself dressed and, after we eat, we be on our way." Being so close to the water, we enjoy seafood as often as possible before winter sets in. Hot coals from breakfast will remain in the fireplace where we'll later roast our bring-home keep of shrimp, crabs, and sometimes oysters. Rusty old cars and some newer models rumble past us on the dusty dirt road. Blaring their horns, some drivers seem intent on reminding us of our humble status. Our hour-long walk to the docks is gratefully shortened if someone offers us a lift.

An old, grey pickup truck pulls alongside us, slowing to a stop. Two farmers emerge from the truck and study us carefully. They own a farm not far from our house. We've learned that white people only engage us when they want something. With predatory precision, in a country drawl, the driver propositions, "Hey, Missy, we wanna give you somethin' for your gal." As they move closer, Mother draws me around behind her, and I cling to her waist. I know enough not to speak. My heart pounds, beating double-time as fear paralyzes me. Standing between the men and me, and understanding their intent, Mother nervously stammers, "No, no, noooo. I can't sell my child." Squeezing me tight, Mother's disbelief transforms her face and furrows her brow as she begins to howl at the dastardly duo. I whimper into Mother's sweaty back as the tramps return to their truck, slam the creaking doors, and drive away.

Unsettled but safe, we arrive at the shrimp dock. Shrimping is a lively time. Adult conversations, manual labor, boats coming and going, and anticipation of dinner make for a full day. The partially-covered shrimp dock transforms into a center of commerce. Fishermen haul in their full nets, laying them out across the long wooden tables for workers to sort. Everyone stands, but my head and hands barely make it above the table, so I stand on a wooden crate to join in the work. Mother and I have our aluminum buckets and wear cloth gardening gloves to safely handle the shrimp. Pulling heads off the bluish-white prawn, we throw the bodies into our buckets and toss the heads aside. We empty our full buckets into a large receptacle and return to the long tables for more. Compensation is a handful of tokens and a supply of shrimp for dinner.

Providing welcome shade, the tallest oaks and pines help us bear the heat and humidity on our long walk home.

* * *

The eldest daughter of three girls, I now live with my mother's youngest sister, Aunt Rosa, and her husband, Uncle Leroy. Leroy Jr. is their only child. No longer will I be spending much time playing with my sisters, climbing trees, or going crabbing with Mother in the tidal pools near our rural stretch of town.

My new home is an electric cold-water flat with two bedrooms and a bathroom. Aunt Rosa works as a domestic for the family that owns the local lumber mill.

Church and school continue to be an important part of my life. The daily walk to and from school seems endless, especially on crispy-cold winter days. The General Store, just past the church on the way to school, offers a welcome opportunity to get in from the freezing cold. Sometimes during lunch and recess, students have permission to buy what they can afford, which is mostly penny candy, gum, saltine crackers, cookies, or an orange soda.

Multiple grade levels are enrolled together at the Robert Smalls School, a one-room wooden schoolhouse for colored children. It was named after an escaped slave who went on to represent Beaufort in Congress. Being older than most of the other students, my fortune is to sit in the rear of the classroom near the wood-fired potbelly stove, the main source of heat in the cold winter months. There is an outhouse a stone's throw from the school.

In later years, I go to the new Robert Smalls School. The more modern building for us colored children has inside plumbing, separate classrooms for different grades, a library, and activity period. School days begin with chapel. Teachers lead students in the reading and recitation of Bible verses. We say the *Pledge of Allegiance*, sing hymns and anthems. I learn clarinet from the short, brown-skinned man teaching music several days per week. I play in the school band and sing in the choir.

My love of children develops naturally. As a teenager, my caregiving after school and during summer vacation helps support the household. Our neighbor, a single parent, supplements her income by bartending in the local tavern after teaching school all day. Her sister is not always available to watch her son, so I care for him until she finishes her second job. Another lady hires me after school and Saturdays to watch her school-age daughter while she tends to customers at the beauty salon. Although it is a segregated community, a white military family asks for my help with their three children over summer vacation.

My joy at being able to purchase necessities for myself without having to ask Auntie brings me a sense of pride, confidence, and independence not previously felt. The certain vulnerability and danger involved with being poor, colored, and female is standard, especially in this rural southern town. I'm thankful for my exposure to many resilient women who have moved beyond their humble circumstances. Successfully educating themselves and pursuing purposeful, meaningful careers as nurses or teachers, they are examples of the upward mobility many in my community seek, despite impoverished, segregated lives with limited opportunities.

One day, a letter arrives requesting I travel to Saratoga Springs, New York at the close of the school year to become a live-in caregiver for Aunt Thelma's and Uncle Chuck's two daughters. They had relocated to Saratoga Springs from my hometown and now need household and child care assistance. After honorably serving his country during World War II, Uncle Chuck tends bar at the Grand Union Hotel. Aunt Thelma is a talented seamstress. For some reason, her education and experience as a teacher in South Carolina does not allow her to secure a teaching position with the Saratoga Springs City Schools. Apparently, New York State has its own set of requirements for teachers and would not qualify her.

My days in Beaufort, South Carolina are numbered. I will be heading north, leaving my family, country life, and everything I've always known in Beaufort, South Carolina. But it seems less daunting to me than one might imagine.

Southern public transportation is segregated, so my ride to the Yemassee train station is with a colored driver via the Brown Cab

Company. Aboard the train, I already know I'll have to switch trains in Philadelphia. Once in New York City, my train will be direct to Saratoga Springs, New York – my new home!

Auntie had reminded me to tip the red cap at the train station. This being my last transfer, I peer into my purse and see the few remaining coins. After reaching in to gather the handful of change, I politely present the tip. The gentleman looks me up and down. Shaking his head with pity, he sharply chides, "If that's all ya got, you can keep it!" In the midst of his crushing rejection, my face flushes hot with hurt. Temporarily speechless, my eyes well up with tears. Switching out my handkerchief for the coins, I carefully count them as they drop back into my purse. I compose myself and look about as the excitement of being in New York City squelches the merciless sting of embarrassment.

The murals, marble, and magnificence of Grand Central Station welcome me with such cosmopolitan grandeur. Everything is delightfully dizzying. The fascinating forms, fashion, and new-found sense of freedom swirl around me. The sights, sounds, and smells of a new life so far from home is almost too much to take in.

I surely do not imagine the excitement and new life that awaits me during my first summer in Saratoga Springs! It's quite the change from a segregated upbringing. Prior to arriving, I know nothing of gambling and prostitution. Living downtown, so close to Congress Street, I am forewarned and soon learn what a Red-Light District is. Despite the excitement of the horse races, new people, and social life I didn't have in the south, my homesickness and depression require that I periodically return to my hometown.

I continue my education in night school, soon realizing that all of my teachers in Saratoga Springs are white. I attend church at the African Methodist Episcopal Zion Church and enjoy sophisticated events, such as the Annual Elks Ball. Aunt Thelma introduces me to Richard, a fine-looking man who lives in the neighborhood. A five-year courtship begins.

Some days, immense sadness and loneliness prevail. I miss Mother and write letters to let her know how I'm managing. I move to New York City to work as a live-in domestic for a well-to-do Jewish family. While there, I take evening classes and graduate from Boys and Girls High School in Brooklyn. Richard's sisters live near-by, so I get to know them, too.

When I return to Saratoga Springs, I marry Richard. Together, we raise three children. I often wonder what my life would have been like had I remained in Beaufort, South Carolina. I left part of myself there and will always be a southern Saratoga soul.

Carol R. Daggs: My mother's story inspires me. I now better appreciate Ruth's history and family foundation in South Carolina. Writing *herstory* has been a creative learning experience and healthy exercise, especially given the craziness in the world right now. Post high school, I received my education at Hartwick College, UMASS Amherst, and the Center for Natural Wellness School of Massage Therapy. I'm a music educator, LMT, and perform as *Jazzage*, artfully applying musical jazz sounds to the auditory apparatus and soul via vocal and instrumental flow. Today, my mother spends time between family in New England and Saratoga Springs, NY.

And the Cardinal Sang
by Ginny Riedman-Dangler

Mary Kay Klee Riedman (1927-2011)

I gather my books and leave the library where I've been working on a short story. I meet up with my friend, Rosemarie, at the bus stop, who grabs my attention with a friendly wave. Together, we board the bus.

"Kay," as she sometimes calls me, "Do you want to go to the RKO Palace tonight? *Key Largo* with Humphrey Bogart is playing."

I reply with an unconvincing, "Sure." What I really want to do is tell her about the job offer I'm hoping to get in today's mail.

"Well, that wasn't very enthusiastic," she responds, looking away.

"Rosemarie, I've been meaning to tell you. When recruiters came to campus a few months ago, I applied for jobs at Gannett Newspapers and Eastman Kodak."

Her eyes light up. "Kay, why didn't you tell me before this? How exciting!"

I hesitantly explain that while I know Kodak employs women for secretarial positions, I'm probably competing with men for a writing position at Gannett. Yet, the job at Gannett is my preference and what I've been working toward for a long time.

Rosemarie looks at me with what-I-perceive-to-be annoyance and says, "Darling, you're more than qualified for the position at the newspaper, more than any male writer. Your writing is exceptional!" As I listen to her, I feel the same annoyance. *Maybe I should have taken a pen name to increase the likelihood of my being given a chance.*

The bus turns left onto East Avenue, adorned with large maple trees and majestic mansions. Tree branches reach for each other over the avenue, forming a magical passage as if welcoming vehicles.

"Rosemarie, thank you for your kind words. I've finally come to believe in myself and my expertise as a writer. I can't think of anything I'd rather do. For now, I'll keep my fingers crossed. And pray, of course."

The bus stops, and Rosemarie stands. She touches my shoulder and says, "I'll say a prayer, too, and, do think about coming to the Palace tonight. It might help to keep your mind occupied with something else."

After hearing Rosemarie's enthusiasm for my work, I can't help but reflect on when my passion for writing began.

I was always a good student, diligent about my assignments. However, I was a quiet child who knew my place. How could I not when the children in our immense home were relegated to the back porch, left to our own musings? After all, it was believed that children were to be seen and not heard. Any dreams my father had for our futures dissolved as the economy became worse. He was diagnosed with Parkinson's disease, which put an additional strain on the family. Eventually, he lost his job, and we had to move into my mother's family home, which was divided into apartments to accommodate my aunts and their families. Being with extended family brought some diversion from the discouragement most of us felt.

In 1940, I earned a scholarship to attend Sacred Heart Academy for young women. I felt so proud, especially given my family's limited income. But then Mother told me I may not be able to attend because she couldn't afford the books and uniforms. My father's Parkinson's was progressing, and costly care was needed. Although Mother was working, her wages were minimal. I was somber for days, not knowing the outcome. Until Father Quinn, the pastor from St. Monica's, came to our door.

He told Mother the parish would pay for my books and uniforms for Sacred Heart. I heard him say, "Mary Kay is bright and talented. She has such great potential, and I'd like to give her an opportunity to succeed." I smiled and breathed a sigh of relief when I heard my appreciative mother respond, "Thank you, Father. We accept your generous gift. We want Mary Kay to succeed, too."

At Sacred Heart, I met Peggy, Coley, and Joan, and we became inseparable. There was the time we left the building after history class to smoke cigarettes behind the grotto. Mother Theresa stopped us and sternly asked, "Where are you going, girls?" With a serious look, but a smiling heart, I curtsied and said, "Why Mother Theresa, we're going to the grotto to say our daily Rosary." She responded, "Be on your way then."

When Peggy and I went to Louie's Sweet Shop one day, she told me about her beau, George, and the complexities of their new romance. George had mailed her a love poem, which her mother had intercepted. Although she thought she was in love, her mother thought her too young to date. Peggy was both angry and embarrassed; she didn't want to lose George over such a faux pas.

I recall this so clearly because I'd been writing my first short story, *All's Fair,* at the time. It was a love story, and I wanted to include a poem I'd written. Hearing Peggy's story gave me the added incentive to include it. Poetry makes romance stories even sweeter.

Although I'd written poetry before, it was my first attempt at free verse. Mother Elizabeth had introduced us to T.S. Elliot, Walt Whitman, and Emily Dickenson. I was so mesmerized when I read their poems. The depth of their words spoke to my innermost soul. My poem, which I had titled *A Thought*, was my way of expressing my sadness as I watched Father's disease progress. His tremors were becoming increasingly worse, and now he was having difficulty speaking and walking. I knew the poem by heart.

How often I have tried all ways
To understand the mystery of your mind;
Searched every corner of my own
To fathom the secret recesses of yours.
Perhaps I am too shallow, too uninspired to inspire you.
Too simple to unchain the complex fetters of a thought - your thoughts,
Which I would make mine - could I but understand.

His suffering still brings tears to my eyes. My life experiences were embedded in my poems and stories.

While boys poured over Superman comics, I was in awe of the new character, Wonder Woman. Her creator, psychologist Dr. Marston, portrayed a strong woman having an impact on the world. The character had a strength I could quietly relate to, a woman with an honorable mission and something meaningful to contribute to society. Certainly, our country needed hope – the mood was bleak.

The academic environment at Sacred Heart was ripe for enhancing my craft. Latin classes expanded my vocabulary. English classes gave me the right foundation to develop sentence structures that coherently expressed my thoughts. Social studies and history classes included passionate discussions of world affairs and ways we, as women, could be of service – if allowed. I sometimes took classroom discussions a step further and wrote small editorials for the school newspaper. I was particularly interested in hearing about the mission and work of Susan B. Anthony. She'd been a *wonder woman* in her time, and her family home was a short distance from mine.

The worldview of significant women such as Eleanor Roosevelt and Frances Perkins also inspired me. They, too, were wonder women. *Could my writing inspire significant, positive changes in the lives of people?*

My idealism and innocence were compromised whenever I read the *Times-Union* or heard adult conversations. Loved ones were being sent overseas to fight in the war, and there was daily news of mass atrocities at the hands of the Nazis. My hometown of Rochester, New York housed many companies that produced for the war effort: Bausch and Lomb Optical, Rochester Products, and Eastman Kodak, to name a few. Parts of warplanes and tanks being made here, and high-grade glass was being manufactured for aerial reconnaissance cameras.

Women were also working on production lines. Mother would bemoan the fact that their pay was typically only twenty dollars a week, half of what men earned. This seemed so unfair to me, especially since this was true of my mother's wages as well.

In 1944, I entered Nazareth College. I had dreamt of this opportunity since elementary school. Any pessimism I heard about this endeavor was based on the question of what I would do with my education after I graduated, married, and started a family. I was also becoming aware of other restrictions and attitudes women were expected to tolerate, which could sabotage my dream of a professional career. Such messages only added fuel to my fire for doing well in school.

I became preoccupied with writing, and there was so much to write about! I had strong beliefs about what was happening in the world and wanted to make a difference. *Perhaps through my writing, I could be heard and make my contribution to society.* Not exactly Wonder Woman but could still make an impact.

My confidence was growing as submissions to *Verity Fair,* the college's literary magazine, were accepted. I was greatly influenced by the prominent journalist, Dorothy Thompson. She was considered a trailblazer for woman aspiring to be journalists and writers, a field dominated by men. Her tenacious personality and outspoken opposition against inhumane war crimes, as well as support for women's rights, inspired me. However, I was also beginning to feel an inner struggle about whether it was permissible for me, as a woman, to express my true, inner thoughts.

It was as if I'd internalized an invalidating societal norm, despite any encouragement and support I had in school. *Was my passion for writing taking on a veil of irony?* I wondered. *I have talent, but would it be safe for me to express my thoughts on controversial issues?* Home economics and child development courses were mandatory for female students. *Could I have a family someday AND a writing career?* I decided not to let any conflicting messages get in the way of concentrating on my studies and pursuing my dream.

When I became literary editor of our yearbook, *The Sigillum,* any doubt about my qualifications as a writer subsided. I kept close to my heart the wisdom and resolve of St. Hilda, which Mother Elizabeth espoused: *You are warrior maidens; be you watchful, indomitable, serene, great-hearted and strong.* Whenever I remembered these words, I was convinced I could accomplish anything.

That was then. But now?

My reverie ends as the bus turns down Genesee Street. The mailman is on Arnett Boulevard walking toward our house. As he walks up the steps to our mailbox, my heart begins to race. *My dream will come true if they offer me the writing position at Gannett. I know I'll do an excellent job!* The bus stops, and I make a quick exit, feeling hopeful.

Peeking into the mailbox, I see two envelopes: One from Gannett, the other from Eastman Kodak. I take a deep breath and, at the same time, hear the sweet song of a cardinal perched on a branch of a maple tree. Unsure which to open first, I hesitantly open the one from Gannett. My heart sinks as I read that they chose an individual for the writing position who has "superior skills." They share, also, that *he* has three years' experience in the field. They thank me for applying and wish me the best as I pursue my writing career.

Disappointment consumes me. The song of the cardinal ebbs as the excitement of the moment ceases. *How can this be? I have experience and a degree.* Tears well up. *Is it because I'm a woman?*

Time stands still as I sink into angry disbelief. The cardinal's new song startles me, and I open the next letter: *We are pleased to offer you a secretarial position in the Personnel Department at the Hawk-Eye Plant beginning July 1, 1948.*

I should be grateful I'm being offered a job. Any job. Yet, my enthusiasm is gone. I am left with ambivalence. I protect myself with rationalizations: *At least I can now help mother with household expenses. Perhaps this position will involve editing, or I'll be asked to draft letters on my own.*

I think back to the final essay I wrote for *Verity Fair,* answering the question *Would You Do It Over?* I'm firm in my conviction that not only would I still have gone to college, but I would take advantage of what college has to offer a girl who wants to make the most of her life – spiritually, socially, and, last but not least, intellectually.

I'll try to move beyond this disappointment. I'll continue to write in some form. The *Times-Union* accepts well-written editorials. Maybe that will get my foot in the door.

I compose myself before going into the house. Perhaps my love of writing will someday be instilled in my children. I quietly place my books on the coffee table and run upstairs to get ready for the movie.

I glance out the window in time to see the cardinal fly away.

Ginny Riedman-Dangler: After my mother's death, we discovered her poems and short stories, which reinforced what I already knew: She was an exceptional writer. But she never had the opportunity to pursue a writing career due to personal circumstances and the limitations women faced. This writing has given me a greater appreciation of her talent as a writer and of her courage and fortitude as a woman. My love of children has inspired my 35-year career as an educator and mental health therapist. Currently, I'm an elementary school counselor in Rochester, NY, where I live with my husband.

Editor Acknowledgements

Many more stories than those showcased were submitted – perhaps someday a Volume II. I'm indebted to the courageous writers who answered the call to submit real-life stories in their foremothers' voices. This is more challenging to do than it may appear. Plus, it isn't easy to expose our family histories; we all have skeletons. But that's the point: We ALL do. Jeannette Walls' books about her family saga helped me see how powerful the truth can be. Shame loses its power over us when presented as universal, relatable human imperfection.

Writers featured in this book conducted extensive research about their foremothers and the times in which they lived. We did our best to ensure historical accuracy. They were infinitely patient with me as I sent them in search of origins of terms, as well as placement in time of events and people. I learned much in the process. For instance, World War I was labeled that after World War II started – prior to that, it was the World War. If only it really had been *The War to End all Wars.*

Saratoga Arts supported my funding request for a Community Arts Grant from the New York State Council on the Arts. I'm proud to live in a state where the arts are valued and funded, not only for their intrinsic aesthetic value, but for their contribution to a cultured society. It's important to protect and support the arts because artists express their truth, thinly veiled at times.

The eight-member editorial board, accomplished writers themselves, blindly judged submissions and made insightful recommendations. The Academy for Lifelong Learning at Empire State College in Saratoga Springs, NY, and literary and women's organizations across the state, helped promote this project. Beta readers, Rick Hasenauer and Leslie Sittner, assisted with fact-checking and, along with Pete Hasenauer, proofread with fresh eyes. Thank you also to those who still read and buy books, who support libraries and independent bookstores. They are sanctuaries for liberty.

Now that we've brought these women back to life, they won't easily return to the recesses of our private memories. The authors in this anthology are highly motivated to continue this project by presenting their stories to high school, college, and adult education classes, as well as to civic, historical, and women's organizations. We live throughout New York State, with roots around the world. For more information about readings, presentations, stocking books, or group sales, contact B4TheyWereOurMothers@gmail.com.

P.A.N
December 2017

Amelia Dembowski Nugent (1915-2004)

Patricia A. Nugent: I didn't realize when I published *They Live On: Saying Goodbye to Mom and Dad,* a collection of vignettes about caregiving and loss, that helping others "live on" would become a theme for so many of my literary endeavors. The early suffragists live on in my play *The Stone that Started the Ripple.* My creative nonfiction essays and poems, paying homage to those who have gone before, have been published in several anthologies, as well as in literary journals and trade magazines. My golden retriever, Dolly, is being immortalized in my current manuscript *Healing with Dolly Lama: Finding God in Dog.* All lives are worth memorializing. I invite you to visit my website at www.journalartspress.com.